WHAT'S WRONG WITH DEVELOPERS?

The truths, myths, and contradictions making software so hard to make.

Bron Davies

Published by Project ICON

Digital ISBN: 978-1-969888-07-6
Paperback ISBN: 978-1-969888-08-3

ICON PUBLISHING HOUSE

https://projecticon.io/

Table of Contents

Chapter 1 – From Assembly Language to Assembling Buzzwords

The software industry has never agreed on what to call the people who build it. Once they were programmers, and now, everyone's an "engineer." The work hasn't changed nearly as much as the titles—just the amount of self-importance attached. Before we can figure out what's wrong with developers, we have to admit we can't even describe them without lying a little.

The Inflation of Titles – What the Title Hides, Reveals, and Distorts

If you ask ten people in the industry to define a software developer, engineer, or programmer, you won't just get ten different answers. You'll also invite three arguments, five contradictory anecdotes, and at least one self-indulgent blog post about "building culture, not code." The industry is so tangled in its own language that the same role might be called Developer I, Software Engineer II, or Full-Stack Ninja, depending on how much caffeine HR had that morning and what headline happened to float across their feed.

At its most stripped-down, a software developer is simply someone who writes instructions for computers. That's it. Whether the person doing it calls themselves a "programmer" or a "solutions architect" is usually less about the scope of their work and more about branding, positioning, and the subtle dance of compensation negotiations. The rest is résumé gloss, corporate theater, and sometimes a desperate attempt to look more important than the actual job requires. Titles, in other words, often obscure more than they reveal.

The industry abandoned any real consistency in titles long ago—if it ever existed in the first place. "Programmer" was considered too generic, too blunt, and maybe even too humble. So, at some point, we borrowed a word with gravitas: Engineer. As if slinging JavaScript carried the same consequences as designing bridges that must stand against earthquakes or turbines that keep hospitals running during a blackout. Using the term "engineer" this way is, technically speaking, tantamount to fraud https://www.nspe.org/nspe-advocacy/explore-issues/professional-policies-and-position-statements/employment-practices-use.

In every U.S. state, engineering in fields like civil, electrical, or mechanical is tightly regulated, guarded by licensure exams, education requirements, and codes of ethics. This is not gatekeeping for its own sake; it's about safeguarding public health, safety, and welfare. No one wants their airplane designed by a hobbyist or their medical device drafted by someone who just "picked up a few tutorials." Yet when it comes to software, there are virtually no barriers to calling yourself an "engineer." You can download a code editor on Tuesday, launch a portfolio on Thursday, and print "Software Engineer" on your business card Friday. No oversight. No credentialing. No shared baseline of competence. While the intent behind using the title may not always be malicious, the effect is to dilute both meaning and trust. Misrepresenting qualifications in this way can have consequences—legal ones, reputational ones, and perhaps most damaging of all, cultural ones that shape how the public and other industries perceive us.

And yet, "Software Engineer" just sounds impressive. We tend to assume, almost without thinking, that someone carrying that title has more skill, more training, or more insight than the average developer. But prestige by association is a poor way of generating value. What we have instead is a kind of linguistic appropriation—borrowing another industry's terminology because it projects more credibility than our own. And once the dam broke, the flood of title inflation was unstoppable.

First came "full-stack developer," because apparently "web developer" didn't sound expensive enough. Then came "DevOps Engineers," "Cloud Evangelists," "AI Prompt Engineers," and countless other contrived combinations designed to suggest indispensability. Every new buzzword represented a tug-of-war between employers and employees. For companies, inflated titles became a way to avoid raising salaries— "we won't give you more money, but we'll call you Senior." For individuals, inflated titles became a currency of self-worth and marketability, proof they were moving up in the world even if their actual work hadn't changed.

On paper, the distinctions seem clear:

- A **programmer** writes code, wrangles syntax, solves algorithms, and gets features built.

- A **software developer** builds applications, integrates systems, and zooms out far enough to consider the bigger picture.

- A **software engineer** steps further back, adopting or designing patterns for scalability, fault tolerance, and long-term performance.

In theory, each role points to a slightly different level of abstraction, a different layer in the stack of thinking. In practice, however, the lines blur until they're almost meaningless. Most professionals end up being some combination of all three, their day-to-day shaped more by the needs of the moment than by their job title. To management, the labels become more about perception than reality.

You can dress up a duck in a lab coat and call it a "waterfowl engineer," but at the end of the day, it still quacks. And in our industry, the quacking is the code. No matter what we call ourselves, the work is measured not by the glamor of the title but by whether the system runs, the app ships, or the customer's problem gets solved. The danger lies in forgetting that simple truth beneath the layers of inflated labels, because when language drifts too far from reality, trust inevitably fades.

A Field Built on Borrowed Terms – from "Engineer" Envy to "Coder" Contempt

Once upon a time, there were programmers. Real ones. The kind who read Knuth not to posture or decorate a bookshelf, but because survival demanded it. They worked in an era when machines could barely render a typeface, and every line of code was a negotiation for resources. Computers were expensive, brittle, and utterly without mercy. There was no "deploy and monitor" pipeline waiting to catch mistakes; if your code failed, it failed catastrophically, sometimes in front of a room full of clients who had just invested their trust and money in the blinking cursor before them. Programmers lived in a world where mistakes were public, brutal, and final.

Their attention wasn't consumed by Jira boards or sprint points. They thought in CPU cycles and memory sizes, in cache misses and disk seeks. They measured cost in milliseconds and bytes, not story points. To them, every instruction carried weight because resources were finite and unforgiving. Efficiency wasn't an optimization; it was the difference between a system running and one collapsing. These were craftspeople who understood, viscerally, that the machine was not their partner but their opponent, an adversary to be mastered through precision, discipline, and an almost obsessive care for detail because deploying an update required a lot more than a push to the main branch.

Then came the hackers, born partly from rebellion and partly from necessity. Hackers were the restless heirs of the programming world, carrying forward the same deep technical foundation but unwilling to be shackled by it. Where programmers submitted themselves to the discipline of hardware constraints, hackers asked: What if those constraints could be bent? They weren't lazy, though outsiders often accused them of it. They were impatient, curious, unwilling to spend a week polishing the "perfect" solution when a clever shortcut could solve the problem in an hour.

To hackers, the system was not a machine to appease but a puzzle to be exploited. Their code often carried a kind of mischievous brilliance, a refusal to play by rules that felt arbitrary or slow. And sometimes, that irreverence led to astonishing breakthroughs. Yet the same quality also left behind brittle artifacts, opaque contraptions that worked until they didn't, and then baffled even their creators. Hackers became legends, their ingenuity celebrated in stories whispered across IRC channels and conference halls. But they also became cautionary figures, reminders of what happens when cleverness outruns sustainability.

For a while, being a hacker was aspirational. It meant you were sharp, inventive, and unwilling to settle for mediocrity. A hacker was a problem solver first and a stylist of code second, someone who treated limitations as challenges to be mocked. They refactored entire modules at three in the morning just to prove it could be done. They lived for the thrill of discovery, chasing the high of making the impossible suddenly possible. But brilliance has a half-life. Hacks that dazzled in the moment often turned into time bombs. Code that had once felt like an elegant exploit became a maintenance nightmare, its cleverness now a liability. What began as a badge of honor eventually curdled into a label of contempt. To be called a hacker became less about respect and more about recklessness.

And then the field shifted again. As software became "easier"—or at least appeared so—and the business world discovered you could build companies atop other people's frameworks, a new figure emerged: the coder. Coders could produce output, and plenty of it. They generated entire forests of Git commits, their keyboards clattering proof of their productivity. But code, abundant though it was, is not synonymous with progress. Coders often knew the syntax but not the system, could copy-paste from Stack Overflow but struggled to grasp architecture or scalability. Their strength was speed, but that speed often came at the expense of understanding.

The problem wasn't just skill but perception. "Coder" sounded too mechanical, too factory-like. It evoked images of sweatshops and conveyor belts, too close to "data entry" for comfort. Coders produced, but the word implied a kind of mindlessness that didn't fit the industry's growing appetite for prestige. Businesses wanted to project innovation, not assembly-line labor. And so, with a shift in vocabulary, coders became developers.

"Developer" carried gravitas. Outside software, developers shape skylines and neighborhoods, molding raw earth into communities. Applied to software, the word implied vision, creativity, even artistry. Suddenly, you weren't just hammering out functions; you were "building the future." It sounded bigger, more serious, less about typing and more about shaping.

In theory, developers were translators, bridging the world of abstract requirements with tangible solutions. They were supposed to consider the business domain, the customers' needs, the constraints of the environment, and then balance all of that into a working system. In theory, they were the grown-up version of the coder. In practice, however, the difference was often cosmetic. Many developers were still implementing specifications without grasping the larger picture. The new title didn't always change the work, but it changed how everyone felt about the work. Employees felt professional, recruiters felt justified, businesses felt visionary. The code itself, of course, remained indifferent.

But the hunger for prestige didn't stop there. "Developer" was aspirational, but not quite enough. So the word engineer slipped in, borrowed from disciplines where the stakes were measured in lives. Civil engineers whose bridges collapse face prison, not just performance reviews. Electrical engineers who design faulty circuits can burn down buildings. The title carries a burden of rigor, ethics, and accountability. It is earned through education, licensure, and the acceptance of responsibility for public safety.

Software, however, imported the word without the weight. A "software engineer" could be anyone whose résumé said so. The worst consequence of failure wasn't lives lost but a system outage, a blown budget, or a scolding during a postmortem meeting. The prestige of engineering had been borrowed, stripped of its guardrails.

It is not uncommon to meet a "Principal Software Engineer" whose greatest achievement is persuading Jenkins to build successfully on the third attempt, or whose grand act of architecture was convincing the team to adopt yet another JavaScript framework "because this one will finally fix everything." The title suggests mastery of resilience and systems design, yet in practice it often signifies salary banding, status inflation, and the corporate desire to reassure outsiders that the work carries a level of rigor it may not possess.

The irony is sharp. Many so-called software engineers operate without the discipline or the accountability that define true engineering fields. The industry clings to the title because it reassures clients and executives, creating the illusion of seriousness. And to be fair, some practitioners do bring genuine engineering principles into software: formal methods, fault-tolerant systems, safety-critical design. But the title itself has been inflated so far beyond meaning that from a résumé alone, you cannot tell if "engineer" means architect of resilient systems or simply "they set up CI/CD once."

What we are left with is a field built on borrowed terms, each title carrying a shadow of envy or shame. Programmer, hacker, coder, developer, engineer—they are not just labels but mirrors reflecting how the industry wants to see itself. Sometimes that reflection is honest. More often, it is theater. And behind the theater, the code keeps quacking, indifferent to the titles we wrap around it.

The Prestige Appropriation – How Labels Fuel Stereotypes and Fail Projects

The (de)evolution is easy enough to trace if you squint:
Programmers once lived close to the metal, knowing the cost of every instruction as if it were written into their bones.
Hackers broke free of those constraints, improvising clever shortcuts and quick wins, for better or worse.
Coders came next, producing endless lines of instructions with wildly varying degrees of functionality.
Developers gained their title simply by participating in the act of shipping something, regardless of scope.

And engineers—at least in software—claimed theirs for prestige and salary, not because they practiced anything that resembled engineering rigor.

What has been lost in this slide is not raw talent, but focus. Early programmers had no choice but to obsess over efficiency, correctness, and maintainability because their environment punished anything less. They knew that sloppy design or wasted cycles could bring down an entire system, and when it broke, there were no guardrails to soften the fall. That relentless demand forged discipline. Today, by contrast, coders can deploy something flashy in a matter of hours, but whether it survives real-world load is worse than a coin toss. The industry has traded precision for velocity, depth for résumé keywords, discipline for expediency. We are now in an age where complexity is at its peak, yet attention to fundamentals has never been lower. Modern systems are more intricate than ever, sprawling webs of dependencies and abstractions, and a superficial understanding can be not just insufficient but catastrophic.

And so we arrive at the present day, where everyone is everything: The "engineer" is also a "developer" is also a "programmer." The distinctions blur until they collapse into self-branding. Titles have become costume jewelry, worn to project an image more than to describe a role. We are not producing better software; we are producing more of it, faster, and trusting the cloud bill doesn't bleed us dry before the next funding round.

The confusion cuts deepest when businesses try to hire. They often don't know which archetype they actually need. If the goal is a quick prototype, they may mistakenly hire a computer science purist who insists on over-architecting every component until the project grinds to a halt. If the goal is to build something robust and scalable, they might outsource to a quick-and-dirty coder on Fiverr, who hands them a house of cards destined to collapse under its first real user base. The misalignment is predictable, and so is the frustration. Companies end up asking why nothing seems to match their expectations when the real problem was that the label they trusted was more illusion than guidance. And lurking around the edges are the vibe-coders—those who generate a kind of performative energy around their work without actually delivering much of substance. (More on that later.)

The obsession with titles hides the truth that the core skill remains unchanged: the act of converting requirements into working software someone will actually use. Everything else—the frameworks, the toolchains, the cloud providers—is flavor, not essence. But titles make it feel as though there are tribes, and with tribes come stereotypes. The "engineer" is serious and methodical, the "hacker" reckless but brilliant, the "coder" cheap and disposable. None of these caricatures does justice to the complexity of what the work requires.

There is, however, a more uncomfortable reality. Not everyone in these roles is particularly good at them. Software development has one of the lowest barriers to entry for high-paying work in history. The market is saturated with people who can write code but cannot solve problems. It is a peculiar distortion: the job market rewards keywords more than competence. Teams get filled with "résumé developers," professionals whose skills are fine-tuned for passing interviews rather than delivering results in the trenches. Predictably, this leads to projects that stall indefinitely, products that collapse on launch, and executives scratching their heads at why so many developers are on payroll yet nothing tangible makes it to market.

This is where the word "coder" took on its new sting. It became shorthand for someone who lacks depth, who has technical familiarity but no real craftsmanship. "Coder" now sounds dismissive, almost insulting, as though the person is doing grunt work that requires no imagination. It suggests a lack of care, a lack of understanding, a lack of artistry. And yet the irony is that most professionals I have met are nothing like that stereotype. The majority are deeply committed to their craft, conscientious about their systems, and motivated not only by deadlines but by pride in their work. Collectively, their contributions since the 1980s have powered an astonishing boom in technology—one that has reshaped every industry, every economy, and arguably every culture on the planet. The fact that such enormous change has been delivered in a single professional lifetime is evidence that much more than shallow coding has been at work.

Experience, then, matters more than title. Veterans know how to navigate the complexities of real-world systems, where elegant theory collides with messy requirements and unpredictable users. They have the battle scars of failed deployments and the wisdom that comes only from watching an outage ripple across a business at the worst possible moment. Their craft is not defined by what is printed on a business card but by their ability to shepherd fragile, invisible logic into robust, enduring systems.

So for the sake of clarity, I am going to flatten the landscape. Whatever the label—programmer, hacker, coder, developer, engineer—I will simply call them developers. It is a simplification, yes, but one that emphasizes the shared foundation of skills rather than the differences inflated by prestige. You may disagree with whether those distinctions should be preserved, but perhaps you can agree that the very act of arguing about them proves how tangled and distracting the conversation has become. After all, what's wrong with "developers"?

Chapter 2 – The Productivity Trap

Somewhere along the way, "productivity" stopped meaning "building good software" and started meaning "working sixty-plus hours a week so a dashboard looks green." The cult of productivity has turned into a treadmill: Run faster, log more hours, check more boxes—just don't ask if any of it actually matters. We've mistaken exhaustion for commitment and busywork for progress, and the result is an industry that talks about efficiency while normalizing burnout as a badge of honor.

Busy vs. Productive – Why Output Metrics Can Be a Dangerous Illusion

For better or worse, the question that echoes in most developers' minds is deceptively simple: "How can I be more productive?" It's not just an internal whisper, either. It's the same question management repeats in meeting after meeting, often voiced without hesitation and rarely without pressure. Productivity has become the shared obsession of both sides of the table. Executives want it quantified, managers want it tracked, and developers want to feel it in their bones. And because developer salaries, tools, and infrastructure represent one of the largest slices of a company's budget, the expectation is relentless. If so much money is being poured into this department, then surely the return should be visible: more features, faster delivery, higher profits. The logic is straightforward, but the reality is anything but.

Let's take a deeper look at this developer-productivity mindset and what it really does to the people living inside of it.

A genuinely productive developer is not the one writing the most lines of code, nor the one committing the most changes in a week. True productivity shows itself in subtler, harder-to-measure ways. It is the ability to consistently deliver working, maintainable software that actually solves business problems instead of just satisfying tickets. Productivity grows out of a cocktail of factors: hard-won skill, familiarity with the domain, clarity of priorities, and—perhaps most importantly—sustained focus without constant interruption. The most effective developers know when to write new code, when to clean up old code, and when to push back on requirements that don't make sense. They conserve energy by refusing to fight pointless battles and instead channel it into outcomes that matter. They shape their environments, minimize friction, and learn how to structure their day so that distractions don't derail them. To outsiders, they may not always look busy. But the value they produce compounds in ways that outlive the short-term sprints.

Unproductive developers, on the other hand, often look the busiest. Their keyboards are clattering, their tickets are constantly in progress, and yet progress feels strangely absent. They can spend hours refactoring code for aesthetic reasons, chasing the elegance of a design pattern that solves nothing. Or they throw themselves into trendy technologies that are exciting to learn but irrelevant to the company's goals. The cost isn't just wasted hours; it's morale-sapping dead ends and discarded work. Sometimes the blockage comes from outside forces: endless meetings, shifting priorities, vague requirements, poor leadership, or clunky tooling. Other times, the bottleneck is self-inflicted: developers who won't ask for help, who insist on reinventing the wheel, or who simply don't know how to prioritize. These behaviors generate motion without movement. Busy, yes. Productive, no. And if we are honest, almost every team has lived through this illusion, watching weeks of effort collapse into nothing when the work is thrown away or rewritten.

This distinction between "busy" and "productive" may sound obvious, yet it is astonishing how often organizations reward the wrong one. The developer who works late into the night patching trivial bugs may be celebrated for their dedication, while the developer who quietly prevents those bugs from ever existing may go unnoticed. The irony is that the second developer—the one who avoids problems rather than scrambling to fix them—adds more long-term value. But because their contribution is less visible, it rarely gets measured, let alone praised.

Part of the trap lies in how developers themselves experience productivity. Developers often *feel* productive when they are visibly active: writing code, fixing obvious bugs, checking off tasks in Jira, or closing tickets in rapid succession. This sense of forward motion is intoxicating. It creates the illusion of accomplishment. But the problem is that activity does not equal impact. A developer can spend a full week wiring up an elaborate logging system or writing dozens of unit tests for trivial getters and setters and feel a surge of satisfaction, even when the business value is negligible.

This is why output metrics—commits, lines of code, ticket completions—are such dangerous proxies. They measure what is easy to count, not what is meaningful. They encourage shallow victories, the dopamine rush of progress without the substance of impact. In some ways, they are the productivity equivalent of fast food: filling in the moment but ultimately unsustainable.

Yet dismissing this "feeling of productivity" outright would also be a mistake. Because in a profession where so much of the work is invisible, where progress often looks like hours of staring at a screen in silence, perception matters. Developers who feel they are making progress are more engaged, more motivated, and more resilient in the face of setbacks. They are more likely to tackle difficult problems head-on rather than avoid them. Without that psychological reinforcement, even the most talented developers can slide into apathy, quietly questioning whether their work has any meaning at all. In an industry where output is intangible and where days can vanish into debugging the invisible, the sensation of progress becomes its own kind of fuel.

The paradox, then, is this: the things that make developers feel productive are not always the things that actually matter, but without that feeling, real productivity is harder to sustain. Organizations that fail to understand this end up with demoralized teams chasing empty metrics, and developers who confuse busyness for contribution.

The challenge is not just to measure productivity, but to define it honestly. To ask not how many tickets were closed this week, but whether the work moved the business forward. To recognize that the best developers may look quiet while they are preventing disasters, while the loudest activity may sometimes mask a lack of progress. And to remember that the line between busy and productive is thin, blurry, and too often crossed without anyone noticing.

The Flow State Mirage – How "Feeling" Productive Differs from Being Productive

Flow state is the holy grail of creative work. It is the mental zone where developers operate at peak efficiency, fully immersed in the problem at hand, undistracted and almost transcendent in their focus. In flow, the noise of the outside world fades to nothing. Hours pass unnoticed, decisions feel intuitive, and lines of code seem to appear on the screen as if the hands were only following instructions whispered directly from the mind. The experience is intoxicating. Developers often describe it as if the code is "writing itself," the barriers between thought and execution temporarily erased.

But flow does not come cheaply. Achieving it requires a delicate balance of challenge and skill—tasks that are demanding enough to stretch the mind but not so overwhelming as to paralyze it. It also requires clarity: a well-defined objective, a direction that is neither muddled nor constantly shifting. And perhaps most importantly, it requires uninterrupted time. For developers, the natural enemy of flow is not difficulty but distraction. The modern workplace has perfected the art of interruption: Slack pings that demand immediate response, daily stand-ups that fracture the morning, "quick" requests from management that balloon into half a day's detour. Once broken, flow is not easily restored. It can take twenty to thirty minutes to re-enter the zone, if it returns at all. Many developers spend entire days never regaining it.

This is hard for those outside of the software industry to understand. Much traditional work is already fragmented, a sequence of smaller, more modular tasks where interruptions do not derail the entire process. In those contexts, multitasking can sometimes feel natural. But programming is different. It demands the simultaneous juggling of multiple abstract concepts: data structures, business rules, edge cases, performance considerations, and the mental map of a system that may stretch across millions of lines of code. To be in flow is to hold all of that complexity in suspension at once, as if balancing spinning plates while sprinting forward. Break the concentration, and all of it comes crashing down. Even small interruptions—the kind an outsider might dismiss as harmless—can be catastrophic to this fragile equilibrium.

The impact of these distractions is not just a nuisance; it is a tax on productivity that compounds invisibly. Developers who are constantly yanked out of flow may work the same number of hours as their peers yet accomplish a fraction of the meaningful output. The average developer is rarely doing just "one thing." Even what looks like a single task is, in practice, dozens of threads of thought woven together. Busy-work—status updates, minor formatting tweaks, reorganizing tasks—might appear harmless on the surface, but each one exacts a toll. Each one burns cognitive energy that could have gone into solving deeper problems.

Here lies the heart of the mirage. Busy developers work long hours, attend countless meetings, and always appear engaged. They are perpetually in motion, their calendars full, and their laptops always open. Productive developers, by contrast, may not look as frenetic. They may guard their time, decline unnecessary meetings, and prioritize rest. Yet they deliver results that matter. The distinction is simple in theory but elusive in practice: Busyness measures activity, while productivity measures impact. A developer can spend an entire week refactoring the same method for aesthetic reasons and be "busy" every hour of it but produce nothing that changes the user's experience or moves the business forward.

Management often struggles with this distinction because busyness is visible, easy to quantify, and easy to reward. Time sheets, ticket completions, lines of code—all give the illusion of control, of measurement. Productivity, by contrast, demands a deeper understanding. It requires leaders to ask harder questions: Does this feature solve a real problem? Does this refactor prevent future failures? Did this week's effort reduce friction for customers, or only generate motion for its own sake?

And so flow, paradoxically, becomes both savior and seducer. When developers achieve it, they feel unstoppable, carried forward on waves of momentum. Yet the feeling of progress is not always aligned with progress itself. Flow can be poured into high-value work, the kind that saves the business millions—or it can be poured into polishing a function that no one will ever notice. Flow amplifies whatever it touches, whether vital or trivial. The danger is mistaking the state itself for proof of value.

The mirage of flow, then, is not that it isn't real. It is very real, and very powerful. The mirage is believing that because we feel productive, we necessarily are. The truth is more complicated. Flow is fuel, but it must be directed wisely. Without discernment, it becomes energy squandered on the wrong road. With discernment, it can be the force that propels a project across the finish line.

Balancing Speed and Quality – Trade-Offs That Can Make or Break a Project

Productivity metrics are a double-edged sword, sharp on both sides and dangerous to whoever wields them carelessly. On the surface, they seem indispensable. They give managers a way to quantify output, to point at numbers and say with confidence that progress is being made. They reveal bottlenecks, expose trends, and help teams feel as though they are moving with purpose. But beneath that surface, metrics also create shadows—perverse incentives that warp behavior, encourage gaming the system, and slowly corrode the quality of the very work they were meant to improve.

The industry's favorite yardsticks—lines of code, commits, story points—are among the worst offenders. They are convenient to track but poor proxies for actual value delivered. Count lines of code, and suddenly verbosity looks virtuous. Track commits, and watch developers break work into a dozen superficial pushes just to inflate their numbers. Emphasize story points, and estimates balloon until every task conveniently fits the metric. Instead of optimizing for the mission, teams end up optimizing for the scoreboard. The result is software that looks productive on paper but collapses under scrutiny: bloated, brittle, and riddled with unnecessary complexity.

Why, then, do we cling so tightly to these flawed measures? The answer lies not in malice but in insecurity. Management loves metrics because numbers provide the illusion of control. For leaders without technical expertise, counting things is comforting. Pull requests, bug counts, hours logged—these look objective, tidy, scientific. Numbers impose a veneer of order on a discipline that is anything but. They allow managers to compare developers, teams, and projects without having to wade into the messy context that makes each unique. A spreadsheet promises clarity, even when what it delivers is distortion.

So are productivity metrics useful or harmful? The answer, like so many in software, is "it depends." When treated as indicators rather than absolutes, metrics can be powerful. They can surface trends, reveal outliers, and act as an early-warning system. But once those same numbers become performance targets, they poison the well. Developers, being clever and pragmatic, will inevitably game the system. They split tickets, inflate estimates, pad commit counts, or crank out verbose code to keep the charts green. Over time, the organization loses sight of outcomes altogether. This is Goodhart's Law in action: "When a measure becomes a target, it ceases to be a good measure."

The list of commonly tracked metrics is long: velocity, code coverage percentage, cycle time, deployment frequency, regression counts, incident frequency, mean time to resolution. They look precise when plotted on a dashboard, but precision is not the same as truth. Most are activity-based metrics—measures of motion—when what companies truly need are outcome-based metrics: adoption rates, customer satisfaction, reduced costs, increased revenue, internal efficiency. Mistaking activity for impact is a dangerous sleight of hand. Worse still, when metrics are tied to individual performance evaluations, they erode morale. Developers stop seeing the point of their work beyond feeding the numbers. High performers resent being judged by irrelevant measures. Lower performers hide behind inflated statistics. Trust between teams and management fractures, replaced by cynicism and quiet disengagement.

Often, this obsession with measuring developer productivity is borrowed from other areas of business management, where output is easier to define. On an assembly line, you can count units. In logistics, you can count shipments. But in software, the output is intangible, creative, and layered. The attempt to squeeze it into tidy boxes inevitably backfires. Burnout rises. Engagement falls. The spreadsheet glows green while the product itself falters.

The overemphasis on raw productivity creates short-term bursts of output at the expense of long-term sustainability. Under pressure to "do more," developers cut corners on testing, skip documentation, and paper over fragile architecture. Every shortcut buys time today at the expense of tomorrow, creating liabilities that grow quietly in the background until they consume entire release cycles. This mindset also breeds presenteeism, where employees work visibly long hours to signal commitment but deliver little of lasting value. In the worst cases, creative problem solvers are reduced to assembly-line laborers, their autonomy stripped away, their work treated as interchangeable. The very people you need most—the curious, the inventive, the disciplined builders—are the ones most likely to leave under such conditions.

And the irony is brutal: The harder management pushes for productivity, the less productive the team becomes. Developers treated like cogs disengage. They do just enough to avoid criticism but no more. Innovation withers. Quality slips. Burnout and turnover rise, placing even greater pressure on those who remain. The cycle feeds itself, a downward spiral powered by good intentions gone awry.

Escaping this trap requires reframing the very definition of success. Productivity is not about maximizing throughput at any cost. It is about delivering the right features at the right time, with the right level of durability. That means slowing down when necessary. It means allocating time for code review, for refactoring, for testing, even if it lowers the immediate velocity. Teams that embrace discipline—managing technical debt, setting realistic deadlines, refusing to chase vanity metrics—tend to move faster in the long run precisely because they are not constantly tripping over their own mess.

Instead of measuring points completed, effective teams measure how well those points align with user needs and business goals. Success is not defined by whether the backlog burns down but by whether the product lifts up the people using it. A holistic approach recognizes quality and sustainability as inseparable from time to market. It cultivates an environment where developers are free to prioritize quality without fear of reprisal, where they understand that every line of code is not an asset but a liability—a risk to be managed. Smart managers know this instinctively: controlling that risk is more important than counting raw output.

True success in software is never about hitting a deadline for its own sake. It is about delivering working solutions that users actually want, that solve real problems, that achieve business objectives. Deadlines and budgets matter, but they are secondary to whether the product fulfills its purpose. The best teams manage to achieve both: Shipping high-quality work on time and within budget, while also ensuring that what they deliver is valuable. That rare balance is usually the sign of a team that not only knows what it takes to build something but also has the maturity to estimate honestly and execute reliably.

Balancing speed and quality, then, is less about choosing one over the other and more about learning to see them as inseparable. Speed without quality creates waste. Quality without speed breeds irrelevance. Success lies in holding the tension between the two, refusing to sacrifice one at the altar of the other. It is in that balance—not in metrics, not in dashboards—that real productivity lives.

Chapter 3 – Metrics, Morale, and Mismanagement

If productivity is the cult, then KPIs are its gospel—preached from dashboards and canonized in Jira tickets, their sacred numbers paraded as proof of progress. We measure what's easy to count, not what truly matters, and then act surprised when developers inflate estimates, ship half-baked features, or burn out trying to keep the charts out of the red zone. The result is not better software—it's progress theater, where the actors are weary and the audience is disillusioned. But let's be honest here: the real issue is not the metrics themselves; it's how we use them.

The Tyranny of KPIs – How Measurement Shapes Behavior and Culture

KPIs were meant to help. A useful KPI might track deployment frequency, time from inception to market, defect rates, uptime, customer satisfaction scores, or time-to-recovery after incidents. On the business side, metrics could focus on user growth, retention, revenue impact, or operational savings. The idea is simple: Measure both delivery capability and value creation—not just activity. When chosen carefully and monitored thoughtfully, KPIs can give a much-needed pulse check on progress. They can uncover trends, highlight strengths, and spotlight areas in need of improvement. The more data we gather, the more likely we are to make informed decisions, to make adjustments, and to understand the direction we're heading.

But as is so often the case, the trouble begins when those metrics stop being signals and start being scoreboards. What was once a tool for insight mutates into a blunt instrument of accountability. Track story points, and suddenly teams begin inflating estimates just to hit the numbers. Track commits, and developers start pushing empty ones, adding tiny tweaks to justify a bigger count. Track deployment frequency, and watch as the team delivers more features, but half-baked, untested, and prone to failure. The problem is that measurement no longer just observes behavior—it actively changes it. Worse still, it rewards the wrong kinds of behavior. Instead of focusing on shipping real value, teams begin optimizing for whatever metric is being tracked, feeding management's dashboard while quietly starving the product.

The tyranny doesn't lie in measurement itself. It lies in the distortion that occurs when we mistake measurement for management. A KPI that was supposed to guide the team toward more meaningful work quickly becomes a tool to manage by the numbers. A dashboard glowing green doesn't reveal the full picture. It doesn't tell you about the messy, human realities behind the numbers. A team hitting every target might still be building the wrong thing or building it badly. KPIs aren't designed to catch this; they don't measure the nuance, the judgment, or the quality behind each decision. They reduce a complicated, creative process into something that fits neatly on a slide deck for quarterly reviews. And that convenience comes at a cost: It erodes trust. It reduces a developer's hard-won craft into a number on a chart.

And yet companies cling to KPIs like talismans. They offer executives the comforting illusion of objectivity, a sense that development can be governed by the same levers as logistics or finance. But software is not an assembly line. It is a living, shifting negotiation between constraints, requirements, and creativity. The act of boiling it down to a handful of numbers guarantees distortion. The numbers may look scientific, but they rarely tell the whole story. In fact, they often tell a convincing lie—a lie that hides the truth behind layers of statistics and charts in management's dashboard.

The most dangerous distortion is the way KPIs shape company culture. When you prioritize numbers over context, you encourage behavior that undermines quality. Developers begin to treat their work like a game—a game in which the rules are rigged to favor numbers over impact. The rush to "hit the numbers" becomes the driving force, not the desire to create something meaningful. As the numbers rise, morale plummets. Developers stop caring about the bigger picture because the system has conditioned them to care only about hitting arbitrary targets.

This creates a vicious cycle. Developers, under constant pressure to perform, cut corners. They ship incomplete features, skip testing, and ignore technical debt—anything to meet the next deadline or tick off another story point. And the results are often catastrophic. The codebase becomes more fragile, more difficult to maintain, and ultimately more costly to fix. Teams become increasingly disillusioned, their work devalued by metrics that reduce their creative problem-solving to nothing more than a number. All of these should be viewed as symptoms of an organization that is managing optics instead of outcomes.

Perhaps the most insidious impact of KPIs is their effect on trust. When metrics are tied to individual performance, developers can't help but feel judged by them. The fear of failure begins to outweigh the desire to innovate, to experiment, to push boundaries. Developers stop taking risks because the price of failure is no longer seen as an opportunity for growth—it's a hit to the numbers. High performers start to burn out, resenting the reduction of their work to a meaningless score. Lower performers, in turn, hide behind inflated stats, avoiding real accountability. Trust between developers and management erodes because everyone knows that "success" is no longer about the quality of the software but about how well they can manipulate the numbers.

Ultimately, the danger lies not in the metrics themselves, but in the way they're wielded. A good KPI should be a guide, a light illuminating the path forward, not a cudgel used to beat the team into submission. And yet too many organizations treat their KPIs as performance targets, as if the numbers on a spreadsheet can tell them everything they need to know. The truth is that no KPI can capture the full complexity of a developer's work or the nuances of the software they build. What it does capture, all too often, is a distorted reflection of what management wants to see. And the result is a culture built on false metrics, where the team is measured by what's easy to count, not by the value they create.

When Numbers Lie – the Hidden Costs of Over-Reliance on Productivity Metrics

The illusion of control that KPIs provide comes with a steep price tag. It's a seductive illusion, one that companies latch onto with fervor. Teams that live and die by the dashboard inevitably start to play the game, driven by the numbers that dictate their fate. If the organization celebrates commits, developers break work into dozens of trivial pushes to keep the numbers ticking up. If the focus is on story points, estimates balloon to fill the space available, stretching tasks to meet arbitrary targets. If velocity is the prized metric, then corners get cut—tests are skipped, documentation is ignored, technical debt is buried under the weight of immediate deliverables. On paper, everything looks fine, shiny even. In reality, the foundation is crumbling, slowly and surely, like a house built on sand.

This quiet cancer often reveals itself in two predictable, destructive ways. The first is technical: Brittle software that collapses under real-world conditions. Optimizing for speed at the expense of quality guarantees that bugs, outages, and rework will consume more time than was ever "saved." The second is human: Developers, worn thin by the relentless pressure to chase numbers, begin to disengage. Burnout doesn't strike with a single, dramatic blow. It accumulates, a slow erosion, as people realize that their best efforts—long hours, sleepless nights, the sacrifices they make—are being reduced to little more than numbers on a slide deck. The pain isn't felt immediately, but it's always there, a quiet undercurrent that drags them down, bit by bit.

The result is software that's expensive twice over. Once, because the team is burning through payroll at unsustainable hours, clocking in overtime just to keep up with demands that grow faster than their capacity. And again, because the code they produce under such pressure—rushed, unrefined, lacking the attention it deserves—has to be rewritten, patched, or outright scrapped. Companies that insist they "can't afford" to slow down, to take time for quality and reflection, will inevitably discover that they've paid for "speed" with interest. The not-so-subtle irony is that what looks like progress on the surface—those green lights and glowing KPIs—is actually debt disguised as delivery. A smooth facade masking a crumbling structure beneath.

The toll is more than just technical. Over-reliance on metrics corrodes the very culture that makes development work fulfilling. Developers who once took pride in their craftsmanship start chasing whatever is rewarded. They quickly learn that management doesn't care whether the feature is useful or whether it truly addresses the user's need. What matters is that it was shipped. Creativity withers under the weight of endless demands, risk-taking disappears, and cynicism seeps into the work. The relentless grind to hit those targets stifles the very things that made them passionate about software development in the first place. What was once an art has now become a rote task, performed simply for the sake of moving the numbers.

In the short term, projects limp along, dragging themselves over the finish line. The KPIs are in line, but the energy is gone, and the spark of innovation has been dulled. In the long term, the damage becomes evident. Talent leaves, disillusioned by the hollow pursuit of metrics over meaning. Systems stagnate, caught in an endless cycle of short-term fixes and shallow wins. The organization wonders, with increasing confusion, why morale is plummeting despite the glowing charts that say otherwise. They are staring at data—numbers that say one thing—while the reality, the human story beneath those numbers, has already slipped through their fingers.

The lie in the numbers is not that they are wrong, but that they are incomplete. They measure motion while ignoring meaning. They reward visible busyness while hiding invisible value. Worst of all, they convince leadership that they truly understand what's happening inside the codebase, when in fact they are staring at shadows. The reality, the nuance, the judgment that developers apply in their craft—

those elements cannot be distilled into a metric. And by the time the truth breaks through—usually in the form of a missed deadline, a costly outage, or an exodus of senior staff—the damage is already done. The company is left holding a stack of reports that look great on paper, but which ultimately tell a story of failure.

It's the quietest of betrayals: Those glowing KPIs promising progress, when in reality, they are little more than distractions from the deeper issues. The metrics have created a mirage—one where productivity is mistaken for value, where output is treated as success, and where creativity and quality have been traded for a system that rewards activity over results.

Aligning Metrics with Meaning – Creating Measures That Serve Both Business and Developer Well-Being

The problem with most KPIs isn't that they exist. After all, measurement is a natural part of any business—a way to make sense of an otherwise chaotic process. The issue arises when these metrics get divorced from the work they are meant to represent, when they become isolated from the reality of what's being built and the effort behind it. Executives want clarity, predictability, and the illusion of control over the abstract art of software development. Developers, on the other hand, want autonomy, sanity, and the space to create without being suffocated by arbitrary targets. Somewhere in the middle of these two worlds, the numbers turn into a proxy war—business clings to them as a form of control, while teams resent them for distorting their real work. Yet, it doesn't have to be a zero-sum game.

Healthy measurement begins when both sides acknowledge what the other actually needs. Businesses need visibility. They need to know: Are we moving closer to our goals? Are customers getting value? Are risks being mitigated, or are we gambling with something that could implode down the line? Developers, in contrast, need metrics that reflect the complexity of their work: space to produce high-quality code, recognition of the challenges they face, and protection from the perverse incentives that arise when measurement reduces them to a set of numbers. When both needs overlap, KPIs stop being weapons and start becoming signals—signals everyone can trust because they are grounded in a shared understanding of what really matters.

The reconciliation between these two worlds lies in designing metrics that link outcomes to process, but without flattening either one. Take deployment frequency, for example. It means something if it's tied to customer satisfaction, not just a raw count of pushes. It's one thing to measure how many times code is deployed, but it's quite another to ask, "How often did we ship features without causing a spike in support tickets or churn?" This question bridges both worlds: The business wants velocity, but the developers want stability. By pairing deployment frequency with customer satisfaction, both sides gain visibility into the work being done—and the results being achieved.

Similarly, cycle time matters—but only if it's paired with data on defect rates or team morale. Speed is important, but what good is speed if the features you ship are riddled with bugs or if the team is burning out in the process? The key is not to chase speed for the sake of speed but to ask whether the speed is sustainable and whether it's delivering value. Businesses want predictability, but predictability means little without quality. Pairing cycle time with defect density helps bring balance to that equation. The business can see that features are moving quickly to market, but they also see that the team is being rewarded for delivering high-quality work.

Even the most basic metrics—productivity, for example—can be measured honestly when we stop reducing it to just "more features." True productivity is about sustaining value over time. It includes the technical health of the codebase, the maintainability of the systems, and the retention of the developers themselves. If a team is churning out features but the code is falling apart under the pressure, that's not productive—it's dangerous. If the developers are burning out and leaving in droves, that's not productive either. By measuring features alongside developer retention, technical debt ratios, and system stability, we move closer to a more holistic view of productivity that benefits both the business and the people doing the work.

This doesn't mean that metrics become soft or subjective. In fact, the best KPIs are grounded in the reality of the work. A good KPI doesn't pit speed against quality or leadership against teams—it makes visible the trade-offs that have always been there. Instead of pretending that the business can have infinite features tomorrow or that developers can work at peak capacity forever, these metrics create a common language for negotiating priorities. They show where the tension lies between speed and quality, between deliverables and sustainability. They acknowledge that both sides must make compromises, but they also offer a way to make those compromises consciously, with the goal of creating better products and better outcomes.

There are several budding frameworks and methodologies leading the way toward better management that applies technology to drive business value like Accelerate and DORA.[4] Ultimately these will guide organizations to better outcomes through coupled performance measurements. Consider these examples of reconciled KPIs that bridge both business and development needs:

Deployment Frequency + Customer Satisfaction
This metric goes beyond simply asking, "How often did we ship?" It asks, "How often did we ship without triggering a spike in support tickets or causing customer churn?" This is a smarter way to measure velocity, one that forces the business to acknowledge the value of stability and forces developers to ensure their releases are stable enough to delight customers, not frustrate them.

Cycle Time + Defect Density
Speed alone is misleading. Pairing how fast a feature moves from idea to production with how many defects it introduces creates a fuller picture of what's happening. The business gets predictability from cycle time, while developers are encouraged to think beyond the ticket to the quality of their code. It's a healthier approach that aligns the incentives of both sides.

Uptime + Developer On-Call Load
The business cares about uptime, as it directly affects revenue and user satisfaction. But the team also needs to ensure that the same three

developers aren't always the ones carrying the burden of on-call rotations. By tracking uptime alongside the distribution of on-call load, this KPI strikes a balance between system reliability and team sustainability.

Feature Adoption + Technical Debt Ratio
Feature adoption is an excellent measure of whether a feature is actually providing value to users. But if that metric isn't paired with a measure of technical debt, you end up chasing vanity metrics while ignoring the long-term costs of neglecting your codebase. This pairing forces a conversation about the balance between building features that matter and maintaining the systems that will allow those features to last.

Retention (Customers and Developers)
Businesses care about user retention because it's the lifeblood of growth. But retention isn't just about customers—it's also about developers. A healthy, sustainable team is critical to creating a product that resonates with users. By measuring both customer and developer retention, you can begin to see how one affects the other. Sustainable customer success depends on sustainable teams, and this KPI aligns both sides toward long-term value.

When KPIs are aligned this way, they stop being lies. They become a mirror that shows both the state of the product and the state of the people building it. Executives get the visibility they crave, developers get recognition for more than just raw output, and the organization as a whole avoids the trap of mistaking motion for progress.

And yet, the real test of metrics lies not in their creation but in their application. Tools like Jira, meant to bridge the gap between management and development, often deepen it. Jira is the most prolific project management tool in software, beloved by business for the metrics, reports, and roadmaps it generates. But for developers, it has become a burden, a bureaucratic maze that values ticket-shuffling over problem solving. Every dashboard, every burndown chart feels like proof to management that everything is under control—while to developers, it's a second job, feeding the machine with updates that have little to do with the work itself. Jira isn't just a tool; it's a symptom of the divide between measuring software and making it.

This is the true test of KPIs: whether they illuminate or obscure, whether they guide or manipulate. Too often, what passes for measurement in software is just another layer of theater—numbers arranged to reassure, not to inform. But when done right, when the metrics are designed to serve both the business and the team, they pierce through the illusion. They reveal the truth behind the numbers: that building software isn't about filling dashboards with green lights; it's about solving problems, sustaining teams, and creating systems that endure long after the theater lights go out.

Chapter 4 – Architecture: Where Vision Meets Overengineering

Software architecture is a Goldilocks problem with a bad attitude. Build too little and the system buckles under real use; build too much and the weight of abstractions slows progress to a crawl. The trick is finding the balance point where the design is "just right"—resilient enough to last, but light enough to adapt. Let's take a look at how teams repeatedly miss that mark and what it takes to get closer.

Overbuilt, Underbuilt, and Just Right – Finding Balance in System Design

Software borrowed the term "architecture" for its prestige and then conveniently forgot the obligations that come with it. In construction, architecture is defined by codes, load-bearing capacity, liability, and rigorous inspections. It's constrained by the need for safety and functionality, and when done right, it serves people and places for generations. In software, though, the term is often reduced to a slide that blesses a rewrite, a diagram that outlives the code it was meant to describe, or a title that converts personal preference into doctrine. What gets lost in the process is the understanding that architecture in software isn't just about being "grand" or "sophisticated"; it's about creating a system that works—today, tomorrow, and into the future. Too often, we mistake ceremony for constraint and status for stewardship, ignoring that most so-called "architecture" is shaped by our organizational structure (Conway's Law, 1968). The only decisions that really count are the ones hardest to change, as Martin Fowler reminds us in *Who Needs an Architect?*

What we're left with is architecture theater—second-system effects rationalized as platform strategy (Brooks, *The Mythical Man-Month*), abstractions sized for résumés rather than reality, and irreversible decisions no one is brave enough to own. The cost is not just technical; it's human. The decisions made today don't just lock in tomorrow's code. They lock in the way teams collaborate, the pace at which features are shipped, and the long-term health of the product.

Architecture is the moment when vision collides with reality, when the ideas of yesterday's whiteboard meet the physical limits of tomorrow's servers. It's the point where abstraction meets the physical world: boundaries, data contracts, latency budgets, failure modes, and upgrade paths. Get it wrong, and you're stuck paying for the privilege. Every feature drags a ball and chain; every incident reveals assumptions that were cemented too early. Get it "too right," and you've gold-plated yourself into paralysis, building for hypothetical futures while today's users wait. The sweet spot in architecture doesn't lie in purity—it lies in proportion. Systems should be small enough to change and strong enough to endure. The best working architectures evolve through correction, not grand proclamations. As Lehman's Laws of Software Evolution assert, complex systems that actually work are almost always the result of simpler systems that worked first (*Gall's Law*). Ignore these truths, and you'll rediscover the second-system effect the hard way: ambition outpacing discipline until the design collapses under its own cleverness.

So how do we avoid overbuilding and underbuilding? How do we treat technical debt as a managed reality rather than a moral failing? And, perhaps most importantly, how can we resist the urge to reinvent the wheel, burning calendars and cash, simply because "it's just easier to start over"? These are the questions we must ask when considering how architecture can work as a joint discipline between technical realities and business needs, forcing every decision to be reversible by default and justified by operating metrics, not just box-and-arrow aesthetics.

Architecture at the Right Scale – from Overkill to Undershoot

In software, balance is rarely accidental. It's usually the outcome of bruises and scars—hard-earned lessons learned through repeated failures. Teams that underbuild often learn the hard way. Their minimum viable product (MVP) works fine for the first hundred customers, but when adoption accelerates, the cracks begin to show. Underbuilt systems fail the first real load test. Developers scramble, patching together quick hacks, adding more memory, aggressively caching, duct-taping load balancers. These stopgaps might buy a few weeks, but in the end, the underlying problem remains. The company is forced into a high-risk rewrite under live-fire conditions, burning customer trust and developer morale in the process. The cost of catching up is orders of magnitude higher than simply building it right the first time.

On the other hand, teams that overbuild often discover their own set of problems. Consider the enterprise that decided to hire a "technical steering committee" to design a platform that would scale for years to come. Eighteen months later, the team had dozens of microservices, a Kubernetes-powered infrastructure, CI/CD pipelines bristling with automation, and a dependency graph that looked like it belonged in a doctoral thesis. What they didn't have was a single customer using it. Their system was beautiful—elegant, scalable, and technologically sophisticated—but it was also irrelevant. The market had moved on while they were perfecting diagrams. They had overbuilt, focusing on a grand vision rather than getting something into users' hands quickly. The cost of delay was a missed opportunity, and no amount of refactoring could fix the fundamental problem: they had built something that wasn't needed yet.

The systems that endure are rarely the most elegant or the cheapest. They're the ones that are "just right" for their context. They carry only as much structure as the business can support, only as much flexibility as the team can sustain, and only as much durability as the users will actually notice. This is not an easy balance to strike. It requires discipline—not dogma. Saying no to the tenth abstraction layer. Saying yes to hardening what already works. Admitting that architecture is not about perfection, but about survivability.

The extremes of overbuilding and underbuilding often stem from decisions made in isolation. When architects and developers operate in a vacuum, disconnected from the realities of the market and user needs, they risk creating systems that are either over-engineered or under-engineered. Developers, living inside the code, are hypersensitive to technical pain—slow builds, tangled dependencies, brittle modules. Their instinct is to eliminate this pain, to abstract away the complexity with frameworks and architectures that make their daily lives easier, even if those solutions come with costs the business never signed up for. Business leaders, on the other hand, see only time, budget, and the scoreboard of customer adoption. They don't care about memory leaks or brittle deployment pipelines; they care that the demo works at next month's trade show.

When these two perspectives fail to meet, overbuilding and underbuilding become rational choices within their silos. For developers, overbuilding looks like "future-proofing"—building infrastructure for scale, flexibility, and reuse before a single customer has proven the product's viability. For executives, underbuilding looks like "speed to market"—pushing teams to deliver a facade of functionality that hides a hollow core. Neither approach is malicious. Both are the predictable outcomes of partial information and misaligned incentives.

The irony is that the cure isn't technical; it's conversational. Teams that integrate architectural decisions with business realities—tying scalability to projected growth, durability to contractual obligations, and maintainability to developer turnover—are far less likely to swing to either extreme. It's not that overbuilding and underbuilding disappear, but they become conscious trade-offs instead of accidental disasters. Architecture isn't just a technical discipline; it's a negotiation between what the system could be and what the business can sustain.

Technical Debt as a Living Organism – Why It's Never Fully Gone

Technical debt started as a metaphor—a simple idea that Ward Cunningham introduced to help us understand the cost of shortcuts in software development. It was a way of framing the reality that, in order to speed up the process, we often borrow against the future, knowing that we will eventually have to pay back the price through extra work later. The useful part of this metaphor is in the math: Borrowing buys speed now, but that speed comes with interest in the form of extra effort for every change, every update, every new feature. The harmful part of the metaphor, though, is the moral overlay—treating debt like it's a stain to be scrubbed away, a blemish that tarnishes the "purity" of the system. But technical debt isn't a stain. It's an integral part of how systems evolve in moving markets. Frameworks age, domains shift, teams turn over, and yesterday's "clean" solution becomes today's constraint.

You don't eliminate technical debt. You service it, you refinance it, or you carry it consciously, acknowledging that it's an ever-present part of the landscape. Debt accumulates in every decision, even the so-called "right" ones. What was elegant yesterday becomes brittle today. What we often fail to realize is that every architecture, no matter how well-designed, is a negotiation with the future. The future always changes the terms of that deal. Pretending you can "pay it all off" is like pretending that your code will stop aging the moment you refactor it. Refactoring only buys you time—it doesn't make the debt disappear. The best you can do is keep it in check, prune the worst liabilities, and ensure that the interest you're paying on the debt doesn't exceed the value that's being delivered.

Think of technical debt as a living organism, one that grows and adapts with its environment. Ignore it, and it festers—growing until every change feels like surgery without anesthesia. Overreact to it, and you waste precious cycles chasing purity—rewriting code that's working just fine simply because it looks old. The trick is to give your product's debt just enough attention to keep it healthy. This means deliberate refactoring, automated tests to catch regressions, and architectural decisions that can flex with new demands. Some debt is even strategic. Shipping a brittle prototype to validate customer demand is rational, especially if you've budgeted the cleanup into the plan. Shipping a brittle prototype and pretending it's production-ready? That's malpractice.

The real issue is that business and technology leaders often treat technical debt like a line item on a budget sheet that should eventually go to zero. They demand that teams "clean up the codebase" without understanding that the codebase is a moving target. Developers, in turn, treat technical debt like a scarlet letter—either hiding it in shame or evangelizing complete rewrites in the name of "quality" without ever tying that effort back to business impact or ROI. Both views miss the point entirely. The question isn't whether debt exists; it always does. The real question is whether the organization is servicing it responsibly—balancing interest payments (the extra effort to change the code) against principal reduction (the targeted refactors that buy back agility).

Successful businesses often ride revenue curves on the backs of "spaghetti" systems—messy, tangled code that's understood and manageable because it directly matches the needs of the market. That messy code may be imperfect, but it's real, it's working, and it's generating value. In contrast, many companies attempt to perfect their architectures at the cost of real-time delivery, only to discover too late that the more polished and "perfect" their systems became, the further they drifted from what their customers actually wanted. We've learned the hard way that wholesale rewrites are often fatal—even when the legacy code looks ugly. You trade working behavior and hard-won edge cases for schedule risk, regressions, and missed opportunities.

Monoliths—sometimes modular, sometimes just large—regularly power durable products because they're stable, observable, and cheaper to reason about at the scale that matters. The most successful organizations recognize that a well-tended monolith isn't just an antiquated solution but a strategic asset that has evolved over time to serve the business. Even large-scale companies like Shopify have evolved their monoliths deliberately, continuing to add value while avoiding the temptation to indulge in the cult of microservices. The broader lesson here is unglamorous, but true: choose boring, proven technology, keep shipping, and pay down the worst debt in place. The business value doesn't lie in perfectly layered architecture diagrams—it lies in behavior, in the tacit institutional knowledge that evolves with the system.

The companies that survive, and even thrive, don't eliminate technical debt. They build habits around it. They document it consciously, making it visible in roadmaps, and they revisit it whenever priorities shift. They treat it less like a moral failing and more like a financial planning exercise. Some debt you refinance, some you pay down aggressively, and some you simply carry because it's cheaper than fixing. The key is not to ignore the debt but to know how to manage it. In this way, technical debt becomes less of a monster in the closet and more of a house pet—sometimes messy, occasionally destructive, but an inevitable part of the ecosystem you chose to live in.

This doesn't mean that all technical debt is the same. It's not about blindly accepting poor decisions. It's about understanding that, at its core, technical debt is a symptom of an evolving system, one that must continuously adapt. There will always be choices that are less-than-perfect, and there will always be trade-offs. But by acknowledging the reality of debt and making intentional decisions about how to manage it, organizations can keep their systems healthier, more resilient, and more capable of adapting to change.

Just like any living organism, technical debt needs to be fed and nurtured, not ignored or worshipped. If we treat it like an unavoidable part of growth—one that needs regular care and attention—it becomes less of a burden and more of a tool for long-term success. The real test isn't in eliminating it, but in understanding how to live with it and how to make it work for you, rather than against you.

The Reinventing-the-Wheel Syndrome – When "Custom" Kills Efficiency

"Custom" is how teams turn preferences into payroll. It's a familiar, almost inevitable scenario: Off-the-shelf tools nearly fit, open-source options are "too opinionated," and procurement processes are "slowing us down." So, development does what it does best—it builds. Weeks later, the company has a bespoke feature-flag service, a homegrown queue system, a quasi-authentication system that almost speaks OAuth, and a dashboard framework that somehow looks suspiciously like every other dashboard framework out there.

The bill arrives, but it's not a direct cost—it's an opportunity cost. Every hour spent re-creating something that already exists is an hour not spent building the things that truly differentiate the business. Reinvention isn't innovation. It's unpriced inventory, an accumulation of technical debt that starts as an investment and quickly becomes a liability. What initially seems like an efficient way to solve a problem becomes an anchor that drags the team into a cycle of unnecessary work, maintenance, and technical compromise.

The drivers behind this decision are painfully predictable. Developers want control. Architects imagine future flexibility, solving problems that haven't even arisen yet. Security teams, ever suspicious of third-party solutions, distrust vendors by default. And executives, well—they prefer the idea of "asset creation" over subscriptions that feel like overhead. Add in a dash of "Invented Here" pride and the myth of "unique requirements," and you have the perfect storm—a justification to rebuild wheels that vendors and communities have already perfected.

But what gets overlooked in this process is the total cost of ownership (TCO) and the bus factor. The idea was to avoid vendor lock-in, yet instead, the team locks itself into their own time, resources, and institutional memory. Every time an expert leaves, every time a bug is discovered, every time a new feature is demanded, the team is reminded that they didn't just inherit the product; they inherited the never-ending responsibility of maintaining it.

Reinvention, at its core, carries a silent surcharge—what I call the wheel tax. It's not just the cost of building the solution; it's the total cost spread over time.

$$\text{Wheel tax} = (\text{build time} + \text{integration time}) + (\text{maintenance per year} \times \text{years}) + (\text{incident cost} + \text{slowdown}) - (\text{license avoided})$$

If you don't model these costs in dollars and calendar time, the "free" option always wins the slide deck.

But there's more. We must also account for the option value—the question of whether the custom solution can be changed later, and at what cost. A plugin with a well-known interface makes adoption reversible, but bespoke protocols create sticky solutions that are hard to migrate from. By the time the organization realizes the cost of reinventing the wheel, it's often too late to turn back. The team is stuck, too invested in the solution to easily pivot to something else.

Having the in-house talent to build something doesn't automatically make it a good business decision to own it. When you "own" commodity capabilities, you don't just pay the upfront build cost. You inherit perpetual obligations: patches, upgrades, compliance checks, on-call support, documentation, integration churn, and the staffing risk when your expert leaves for greener pastures. This ownership diverts precious development cycles away from product differentiation and forces the team to wrestle with undifferentiated heavy lifting. It lengthens lead times, raises risk, and shifts the focus from value-creating work to maintaining the very thing that should be enabling value creation. This is the opposite of what executives actually want.

The disciplined approach is "buy/adopt by default, build only where it creates a defensible advantage." This philosophy is grounded in standards that make vendors swappable, and decisions that remain reversible whenever possible. The decision to build custom solutions should be a conscious one, backed by solid reasoning and clear business goals. Put simply: The presence of capable developers is not a license to manufacture liabilities. It's a reason to deploy their talents where the market will notice, where they can create real, sustainable value.

Before jumping into custom development, teams should ask themselves a series of questions:

- **Are we building only where it creates a defensible advantage customers will pay for?**
- **What evidence makes our requirements truly unique? Can we cite a contract, regulation, or hard latency budget? If not, are they actually unique?**
- **How will this custom choice impact operating metrics (lead time, change-fail rate, MTTR, on-call hours)?**
- **Is this a reversible "two-way door" decision? Have we adopted before building and created a seam for future migration?**
- **Are we anchoring on open standards/protocols so vendors are interchangeable, rather than building a foundation that locks us into a specific solution?**
- **Does using a working, supported service today deliver more time-to-value than pursuing a "perfect" in-house solution later?**

Custom is only warranted when it meets all three criteria: (1) it's on the critical path of product differentiation, (2) off-the-shelf options cannot meet a verified constraint (cost at your scale, latency at your edge, a hard regulatory boundary), and (3) you can staff it sustainably for the system's lifespan. Even then, the architecture should be designed with exits in mind: isolate it behind an interface, document the "make or buy" decision, set a review date, and define the metric that must improve to justify continued ownership.

Otherwise, treat custom development like hazardous material—handle carefully, label clearly, and store as little as possible. The uncomfortable truth is that most teams don't need originality; they need throughput. Reinvention flatters our self-image but drains our schedules, our sleep, and our users' patience. The business pays twice: once to build the wheel, and again to rediscover why the old one had spokes.

Discipline—not novelty—is what makes software possible at scale. The temptation to reinvent often comes from a desire to "improve" or "optimize," but these pursuits often come at the cost of real, measurable progress. Save the cleverness for the parts customers can see.

Who Invented Whom? – Why developers Can't Help but Reinvent the Wheel

Open-source's greatest strength—permissionless creation—also guarantees reinvention. Given enough time and enough bored developers, every solved problem acquires five "new takes," each one nudging a slightly different philosophy, license, or API surface. The result is a buyer's market that looks more like a flea market: dozens of nearly identical options, each claiming to be the "standard," and all of them fragmenting attention and maintenance. Randall Munroe captured this dynamic perfectly: when there are "14 competing standards," someone proposes "one universal standard," and suddenly there are 15 standards.

At ecosystem scale, this confusion becomes more pronounced. The Cloud Native Computing Foundation, for example, maintains an interactive landscape cataloging cloud-native projects and products across dozens of overlapping categories—service meshes, ingress controllers, tracing stacks, schedulers—each with multiple contenders (landscape.cncf.io). The map is useful because the space is so crowded that teams need a guide to pick a direction. It also serves as a reminder that "choice" multiplies integration risk, staffing overhead, and migration paths the moment requirements change.

Forks turn reinvention into parallel universes. Elastic's 2021 license change created a clean split: Elasticsearch moved to Elastic License v2/SSPL, while OpenSearch continued as an Apache-licensed fork of 7.10. The result? Two similar stacks with diverging plugins and a long tail of, "Which one do you mean?" in documentation and job postings—a textbook case of market confusion born from governance, not technology.

At the other end of the spectrum, the JavaScript package ecosystem shows how micro-reinvention fuels macro-fragility. The 2016 "left-pad" incident—where one developer unpublishing 11 lines of code used transitively by thousands of packages—briefly broke builds across the entire industry. It forced registries to change policies, highlighting the vulnerability of a system reliant on countless small, reinvented wheels. The lesson wasn't that tiny libraries are bad; it was that when reinvention becomes trivial, dependency graphs become opaque, and operational risk multiplies.

None of this is an argument against open-source software. It's a call to avoid fragmentation and undisciplined adoption. The presence of multiple options is not inherently a virtue; it's a signal to slow down and evaluate the trade-offs. The discipline lies in anchoring on standards, preferring widely adopted projects with healthy communities, and treating every new dependency as a long-term commitment. Every library you add is a bet on its maintainers, its ecosystem, and your team's ability to keep up with its changes. When you multiply that by dozens of dependencies, the risk compounds. The more you rely on open-source, the more you need to manage it like a portfolio—diversifying risk, monitoring health, and pruning liabilities before they become crises.

Chapter 5 – The Contradiction Crisis

Software development thrives on contradictions, and the longer you work in the field, the more you come to realize that these opposites aren't just common—they're inevitable. Every day, developers are bombarded with competing principles, each one claiming to be the truth. We praise simplicity as the highest virtue, quoting Leonardo da Vinci's maxim, "Simplicity is the ultimate sophistication," and yet, we spend most of our time wrestling with frameworks that add complexity by the truckload. Simplicity, it turns out, is often both the goal and the enemy. The simpler a solution is, the more it constrains you. But the more complex a solution is, the harder it is to maintain. It's a constant, ever-present tug-of-war, and somehow, we have to find a way to pull both ropes at once.

Opposites Can Both Be True – the Paradoxes Every Developer Lives With

It's not just about simplicity versus complexity. Technical debt, that ever-present shadow, is another paradoxical force. We're told to minimize it, to reduce its impact and avoid the recklessness of "quick fixes" that accumulate over time. But at the same time, technical debt is celebrated as a necessary evil. It's an unavoidable part of the process, a way of moving quickly to seize market opportunities. Developers constantly hear the same refrain: "We need to move faster, even if it means taking on a little debt." It's a reality of the business world, where speed often trumps purity. So, we carry our debt, and sometimes, we even justify it. After all, if we don't take on debt, we may miss the opportunity that could have been ours. But the cost of that debt grows, slowly, like interest on an unpaid loan, until it becomes a monster we can no longer ignore.

Refactoring—perhaps the most common act of a developer—brings its own paradox. On one hand, it's the sign of a responsible craftsman, someone who cares about the integrity of their work and is willing to invest the time to make it right. But on the other hand, refactoring is also a defense mechanism, a way of avoiding real work. It's easy to justify refactoring when you're faced with a messy codebase, but it can also be an excuse to delay harder, more meaningful tasks. Refactoring is both the solution and the problem, and in the hands of the wrong person, it can become a never-ending cycle of improvement without progress.

Take Agile, for instance. Initially conceived as a rebellion against heavyweight processes, Agile promised adaptability. It was a movement built on the belief that change could be embraced without chaos, that flexibility could coexist with order. Yet, over time, Agile itself became a system of rigid ceremonies. Scrum, a methodology meant to streamline development and enhance collaboration, has often evolved into just another set of bureaucratic rituals that developers must endure. The very thing that was designed to bring freedom has, in some cases, locked teams into a series of meetings and sprints that feel more like the traditional waterfall systems they were meant to replace. Agile, like every other methodology, is not a cure-all—it's both the answer and the problem.

Then there's DRY—Don't Repeat Yourself. It's the mantra of efficient, maintainable code. But as with all good intentions, it eventually becomes problematic. DRY can lead to abstractions that are too brittle. In its desire to reduce duplication, DRY can create dependencies that ripple across the entire codebase. A change to one small part of the system can cause a cascade of changes that no one saw coming. So, while DRY strives to eliminate redundancy, it can also create a more fragile system, one that is harder to modify and more prone to errors. The more we try to eliminate duplication, the more we inadvertently couple the very parts of the system that need flexibility.

Object-oriented programming (OOP), once hailed as the shining star of software design, is itself an embodiment of paradox. At its best, it provides elegant structure to chaotic systems. It encourages encapsulation, modularity, and the ability to reuse code. But at its worst, it entombs systems in rigid hierarchies, where classes are inherited rather than composed, and flexibility becomes a distant dream. OOP promises structure but often delivers a maze of abstract layers that no one can easily navigate. What was once praised as an organizational tool becomes a tangled mess of inheritance, with code that's so tightly coupled that any change feels like unearthing a buried treasure that's been lost for decades.

Even functional programming, the conceptual counterweight to OOP, has its contradictions. It's celebrated for its clarity and purity, and for the ease with which it allows you to reason about code. Yet, many developers dismiss it for its complexity, abstraction, and sometimes convoluted syntax. It's praised by some for its mathematical elegance but dismissed by others for the very same reason. What's clear to one team is an abstract puzzle to another. Functional programming provides solutions for some of the industry's most difficult problems, but it also creates its own set of challenges, pushing the boundaries of abstraction to levels that can leave developers scratching their heads and wondering if it even matters how we categorize our methodologies.

Developers live inside these paradoxes every single day. They constantly navigate these contradictions, trying to keep things simple while also mastering complexity. They try to minimize technical debt, only to realize that it's a necessary part of progress. They refactor, only to end up with more work than they started with. They embrace Agile but sometimes feel trapped by the very processes that were supposed to liberate them. And all the while, they're trying to find balance—between speed and quality, between innovation and stability, between the immediate needs of the business and the long-term goals of the system.

The problem isn't that contradictions exist in the software world. The problem is that we pretend they don't. We act as if the principles we've adopted are universal truths, when in fact they're just local optimizations—solutions that work in some cases but not in others. We embrace dogma because it's comfortable, because it promises clarity, even when the reality is far messier. And in that gap between tidy principles and messy reality, software becomes harder to make.

What makes software development so difficult isn't the absence of principles; it's the fact that every principle has an equally valid opposite that must be considered. The job of a developer isn't to choose one side of the contradiction once and for all; it's to navigate these paradoxes, to learn when to embrace them and when to reject them. It's about moving forward without allowing dogma to masquerade as wisdom.

The crisis we face as an industry isn't the presence of these contradictions—it's our refusal to acknowledge them. We can't eliminate them, but we can learn to live with them. And in doing so, we create better software, not by avoiding paradox, but by embracing it. By accepting that sometimes the right answer is the one that feels uncomfortable, the one that challenges us to think critically about what we truly need and why. In this world of paradoxes, perhaps the most valuable skill a developer can have is the ability to sit with the tension, to find balance in the chaos, and to keep moving forward even when the path ahead is not clearly defined.

When Best Practices Backfire – the Routine Effects of Double-Edged Swords

The developer community thrives on commandments. These aren't the Ten Commandments, of course, but principles passed down from the greats, ideas that seem self-evident and universally applicable. "Don't Repeat Yourself" (DRY). "Follow the Agile Manifesto." "Embrace Object-Oriented Design" (OOP). These mantras were born from a desire to eliminate pain points that plagued software development. DRY was meant to rid us of the inefficiencies that come from repeated code, Agile was a rebellion against the rigidity of Waterfall, and OOP was supposed to bring clarity and structure to messy codebases. All noble intentions. Yet, in practice, these ideals often create the very problems they were meant to solve.

Take DRY, for instance. On paper, it's unimpeachable—eliminate duplication and reduce maintenance overhead. But in the wild, DRY doesn't always play out as expected. What starts as an attempt to simplify and reduce repetition can quickly metastasize into over-abstraction.

Developers generalize too early, coupling domains that have no business being connected, all in the name of avoiding duplication. A “shared” utility is introduced for the sake of DRY, but its only commonality is the label, not the function. Suddenly, a change meant to fix a bug in service A breaks service B in production. And at that moment, the wisdom of avoiding duplication feels like a burden rather than a blessing. DRY’s counterpart, WET ("Write Everything Twice"), is often derided, but in some contexts, it’s the saner approach. Local duplication, when handled properly, is often cheaper and easier to manage than a sprawling global abstraction. Sometimes, the simplest solution is the best, even if it means repeating code.

Or consider Object-Oriented Programming (OOP). It promised to bring order to chaos—objects, inheritance, polymorphism—a model of clarity that mirrored the real world. But in practice, the map rarely matches the terrain. Real projects don’t always fit into neat, textbook hierarchies. The beauty of inheritance becomes a burden, as inheritance chains grow like weeds, each base class modification triggering a cascade of regressions that no one saw coming. What was meant to reduce complexity ends up obscuring it. Abstractions proliferate, leaving developers spelunking through layers of code, ten levels deep before they can figure out where the behavior they need actually resides. The very system that was supposed to make things clear becomes a maze, and suddenly, what seemed like a tool for understanding becomes a tool for confusion. OOP, at its worst, doesn’t deliver clarity—it delivers a mess of indirection.

Agile, the darling of modern software development, is perhaps the most ironic of all. Born out of a desire to escape the rigidity of Waterfall, it promised adaptability and flexibility. Yet, over the years, Agile has morphed into its own bureaucratic machine. Scrum ceremonies, once meant to facilitate collaboration and continuous improvement, have devolved into mere rituals—stand-ups that feel like status theater, sprint planning sessions that turn into estimation poker games, and retrospectives that somehow never lead to real change. Agile was meant to empower teams to embrace failure and learn quickly, yet so often, it becomes another set of processes to follow. Teams are told to “fail fast,” but they’re rarely given the time or resources to learn from failure. The language of Agile—velocity, burndown charts, and more velocity—becomes a new form of measurement, a set of chains disguised as freedom. The promise of agility, once a radical departure from tradition, becomes just another cycle of predictability and process for the sake of process.

The backfire isn't in the principles themselves—it's in the way they've hardened into dogma. A best practice applied universally, without context or discernment, stops being a practice and becomes a liability. DRY is good until it leads to a brittle, overcomplicated system that no one can modify. OOP is valuable until it turns the codebase into a convoluted mess of inheritance chains. Agile feels liberating until it becomes a treadmill of endless rituals that sap the creativity it was meant to foster. Every so-called best practice, when applied without judgment, can backfire. Tools, no matter how revered, can cut the wrong way when wielded blindly.

The uncomfortable truth is that "best practices" should be better understood as "defaults until proven otherwise." They capture lessons learned from past failures, but they aren't guarantees against future ones. In the real world, the same principle that saves one team can ruin another. The difference lies not in the rule itself, but in the developer's ability to assess context and know when to bend, break, or ignore it entirely.

The software world is riddled with catchy slogans—snappy phrases that promise clarity and direction, but which too often get treated as inviolable truths. Some of these slogans began as practical advice, others as rallying cries for change, but all of them are repeated so often that they start to lose their meaning. They've become mantras, mantras we repeat without context, without reflection, without real understanding of when and why they should apply. Here are some of the most common maxims you'll encounter, whether on conference slides, in blog posts, or in the hallways of development offices:

YAGNI (You Aren't Gonna Need It) – A principle that advises against building features until they're truly necessary. Great in theory, until you find yourself in production with a feature you never built, and now you actually do need it.

KISS (Keep It Simple, Stupid) – Simplicity beats cleverness, they say. But "simple" is often in the eye of the beholder, and many developers "simplify" their code into unreadable hacks, burying the complexity under a veil of assumed clarity.

Fail Fast – Surface errors early, they tell you. But sometimes, all this leads to is a loud crash in front of your users, rather than a graceful learning process.

Move Fast and Break Things [1] – Facebook's old mantra. It encourages iteration but often ends up breaking trust along with the software itself, leaving a trail of frustration in its wake.

Release Early, Release Often – The gospel of open-source software. It works until your user base starts to feel like unpaid QA, testing every release with their own time and patience.

Convention Over Configuration – Rails made this a mantra, reducing boilerplate. But what happens when your use case doesn't fit the convention, and now you're wrestling with a framework that feels like it's more trouble than it's worth?

Composition Over Inheritance – A corrective to OOP excess. Good advice, but too often interpreted as "never use inheritance," swinging the pendulum so far that you lose the benefits of a well-designed inheritance structure.

Premature Optimization is the Root of All Evil – Donald Knuth's timeless advice. True enough but misused as an excuse to ignore performance entirely until your system is already on fire.

Make It Work, Make It Right, Make It Fast – Kent Beck's sequence of priorities. Usually applied as "just ship it," with the "make it right" phase quietly skipped.

Automate Everything – CI/CD culture's battle cry. Fantastic, until your build pipeline becomes more complex and fragile than the product it was meant to support.

If It Hurts, Do It More Often – The advice for tasks like deployments or merges. Wise in moderation, masochistic in excess.

Code is Read More Than Written – A call for clarity. But when does clarity become nitpicking? How many code reviews turn into endless debates over brace placement rather than meaningful feedback?

There Should Be One—and Preferably Only One—Obvious Way To Do It – Zen of Python's ideal. Except when there isn't, and Python's many async models and packaging tools make that clear.

Tests are Documentation – A lovely ideal, until your tests become more like crime scene notes—outdated, incomplete, and hard to interpret.

Don't Reinvent the Wheel – Unless, of course, the wheel doesn't quite fit your car, in which case every team happily rebuilds it, convinced they can do it better than everyone else.

These principles, though well-intentioned, are rarely one-size-fits-all solutions. They're tools—good ones, most of the time—but tools that need to be wielded with wisdom, context, and discernment. The irony of "best practices" is that they can often be the most dangerous when they're applied rigidly and universally. The developer's real skill isn't in following the dogma; it's in knowing when and how to adapt these principles to fit the real-world challenges they face, and when to discard them entirely.

Why Dogma Is the Enemy of Good Code – Flexibility as the Ultimate Skill

Rules exist because someone, at some point, got burned badly enough to write them down. These are the lessons learned in the heat of battle—principles that were supposed to make things easier, faster, better. But here's the catch: Clinging to these rules blindly doesn't prevent new burns—it just guarantees them in different places. The truth is, flexibility—the ability to know when to bend the rules or even break them—is what separates competent developers from great ones. And it's also what keeps businesses from wasting months, even years, on purity projects that looked amazing in blog posts but delivered nothing but frustration in practice.

There's a paradox at the heart of software development. Sometimes, the best code isn't the cleanest, most elegant solution. It's the code that shipped fast enough to capture the market and prove the product's value. A brittle prototype in production, for instance, might horrify purists, but if it validates customer demand and brings in revenue, it bought the business time to clean it up later. In contrast, sometimes the right business move is to slow down and resist the urge to "just ship it." Sometimes, it's about taking the time to invest in testing or refactoring, even if it means missing a deadline or letting a product iteration sit longer than planned. That single defect, if left unchecked, could torpedo a contract, sour a relationship, or irreparably damage a user's trust. Either decision—shipping fast or slowing down to improve quality—can feel like heresy, depending on which rulebook you're reading. But both choices can be correct, depending on the context. That's the paradox developers live with: the right answer isn't always obvious, and neither is the rule to follow.

Breaking the sacred "Don't Repeat Yourself" (DRY) principle, for instance, by allowing a bit of duplication might be exactly what a team needs to avoid spending weeks abstracting code that doesn't yet serve a clear purpose. Skipping a sprint ceremony—whether it's a stand-up or a retrospective—might feel wrong in an Agile environment, but for a team that's grinding away on a tight deadline, that hour saved can be the difference between shipping and not shipping. Opting for a monolithic architecture rather than diving headfirst into a distributed microservices setup might raise eyebrows at a board meeting, but for a small team with a tight budget, the monolith might be the most pragmatic choice to keep complexity in check until growth justifies the pain of microservices.

What separates the good from the great isn't the adherence to one principle over another, but the ability to discern when to break the rules and do so strategically. The teams that thrive are the ones who recognize that rules are tools, not commandments. They understand that flexibility isn't about abandoning principles—it's about knowing when a given principle is right for the moment and when it's not.

This is where business and R&D actually converge. Businesses don't care about whether the architecture is "pure," or if the code follows every best practice. They care about whether the system works reliably enough to keep customers satisfied and whether it's cheap enough to maintain in the long run. Developers, on the other hand, don't care if a principle was enshrined in a manifesto twenty years ago. What they care about is whether following it makes today's code easier to understand, modify, or scale. The moment both sides embrace flexibility, when dogma gives way to pragmatism, the tension between business and development resolves. The decisions get made with an eye on what works, not on what looks best on a slide deck.

The irony, of course, is that breaking the rules often looks reckless, but it's usually the more responsible act. Dogma says, "Never deploy on Friday," but a Friday deployment that saves a customer from churn caused by a defect could very well be the better decision. Dogma says, "Test everything," but sometimes a quick one-off script that no one will ever touch again doesn't need a full suite of tests. Dogma says, "Never rewrite," but sometimes the cost of maintaining a rotting legacy system outweighs the risks of starting fresh. What looks like heresy to a purist is often the best choice when you focus on outcomes instead of appearances.

Flexibility in this context isn't about disrespecting principles. It's about respecting the reality of the present situation. The best developers—and the healthiest companies—aren't the ones that follow the rules most consistently. They are the ones who know when and how to break those rules for the right reasons. They understand that the best solutions often lie in the tension between two seemingly opposing forces, and that flexibility is what makes navigating that tension possible.

The paradoxes that define software development aren't going away. Best practices will continue to collide with the messy realities of the work. Commandments will contradict each other, and developers will always be asked to move fast while also ensuring that nothing breaks. The industry's mistake, however, is pretending that these rules are laws of physics, immutable and absolute, when in reality they are trade-offs written in pencil. It's not that developers are incompetent or that businesses are shortsighted. The real issue is that both sides continue to reach for certainty in a discipline that only rewards adaptability.

The job isn't to memorize the commandments. It's knowing which ones to ignore when they get in the way of the work. Flexibility is more than just a developer skill—it's survival in a world that moves too fast to follow rigid dogma. But flexibility only works if it's shared. The ability to break rules responsibly depends on trust—trust between business leaders and the developers writing the code. Trust that business leaders will understand why developers need time to refactor or why a seemingly inefficient decision may actually be the best move in the long run. Trust that developers will know when to push back on what feels like a needless complication, and when to swallow their pride for the sake of delivering something valuable.

That trust is built, and it's tested, in communication. It's in the conversations where developers explain why duplicating a few lines is safer than abstracting them, where product managers articulate the hard deadlines that cannot be moved and the flexible ones that can, and where leaders admit that velocity charts don't capture the full value of what the team is delivering. Without that transparency, dogma fills the void, and best practices harden into brittle constraints that no one dares challenge. And that's when the real crisis begins—not in the code, but in the conversations around it. The crisis isn't in the technology itself, but in the stories we tell ourselves about it, and the assumptions that quietly slip through the cracks, unexamined, until they become roadblocks.

Chapter 6 – Communication: The Missing API

Software development doesn't usually fail because the code is wrong. It fails because the people behind it can't talk to each other. Business speaks in outcomes—growth, market share, profit margins. Developers speak in constraints—latency, throughput, test coverage. And the translation layer between these two worlds? It's often static, riddled with gaps, and breaks in production every single day.

Lost in Translation – Why Developers and Non-Technical People Talk Past Each Other

At the core of every software project is a chain of interpretation. It begins with a business leader: "We need a feature that helps us win more customers." A noble goal, right? But by the time that idea trickles through product managers, designers, and eventually reaches developers, it's been rephrased, reframed, and dissected into something almost unrecognizable. "Build an onboarding flow with an animated wizard and OAuth integration," says the ticket. It's a task now, not a vision. Each step along the way makes sense in isolation, but by the time the feature is delivered, the original business intent is often lost in translation. What started as a simple idea—helping the company win customers—ends up as a narrower, more technical concept. The very thing that was supposed to drive the business forward is now just another line in a sprint backlog. It's no longer about growth; it's about a login button that works.

And that's where the problem begins. Vocabulary. The languages we speak. Business leaders want the quick answers: "Will it work? How long will it take? Will it make money?" Developers, on the other hand, think in terms of complex dependencies, possible failure points, and the risk of something breaking down in the future. Ask a developer when a feature will ship, and they won't give you a date. Instead, they'll tell you that, "It depends. It might work if X happens, but Y could break it, and Z is still untested." It's honesty, maybe even transparency. But to a business leader, it's just an excuse. Developers are trained to hedge their words. To evaluate every possible edge case. But executives, on the other hand, are looking for certainty. They want assurances, not ambiguity. In their world, a deadline is a promise, and any deviation feels like failure. In a meeting between these two worlds, it often feels less like a conversation and more like a hostage negotiation. One side wants promises, and the other wants space to deal with the inherent risk of their work.

Granularity is another issue. Non-technical stakeholders often want summaries: "Will this feature work? When can we expect it?" Developers, though, are trained to dig deep. To evaluate every tiny part of the system before committing to an answer. When a developer says, "It depends," they mean it. They're not being evasive—they're being thorough. But to someone with a more business-oriented mindset, "It depends" translates to "You're stalling." It's a communication breakdown, a failure of language and intent. The truth—that software is inherently probabilistic, full of risks and uncertainties—gets buried between two entirely different worlds. One side wants certainty, and the other embraces uncertainty as part of the process.

This gap in communication is only made worse by the incentives that drive both sides. Executives are rewarded for certainty. They're expected to set clear roadmaps, commit to timelines, and make promises to investors or customers. Developers, however, are rewarded for facing the brutal reality of the code—the late-night debugging, the firefighting when the system crashes under load, the constant vigilance against unseen bugs. When incentives are diametrically opposed—certainty versus embracing the unknown—every conversation becomes a clash of paradigms.

Misalignment becomes the default. Deadlines are missed not because developers are slacking off, but because the estimates given to management were never intended to be guarantees. Features fail to match customer needs, not because developers weren't listening, but because the requirements themselves had already morphed into assumptions by the time they reached the development team. Check-ins and status updates only scratch the surface; they rarely dive into the real reasons why things go wrong. Documentation is supposed to bridge the gap, but it often ends up being written in jargon that only one side understands—or worse, it's ignored entirely.

Some organizations attempt to solve this issue by adding "translators" into the mix—product managers, technical program managers, business analysts—people who are fluent in both dialects. The best translators don't just translate words, they translate priorities. They understand that "must ship by June" isn't just an arbitrary deadline, but it's tied to an upcoming renewal contract. They can also explain to business leaders that "three months of refactoring" isn't a delay, it's necessary to prevent a future support nightmare that will cost more than the contract is worth. Without this bridge, each side keeps shouting in its native tongue, convinced that the other side simply doesn't understand. In the absence of good communication, dogma takes hold—"best practices" harden into rigid constraints, and neither side dares challenge the other.

This translation process isn't optional in software—it's part of the job. Building the wrong thing faster doesn't help the business. Building the right thing too slowly doesn't help either. The art of software lies in turning ambition into constraints and constraints into commitments—without either side feeling deceived. Until that becomes a discipline, software projects will continue to fail—not because of the code, but because of the conversations surrounding it.

And so, the real challenge of software development isn't in the code. It's in the conversations. It's in translating between the worlds of business and development, where different languages and priorities collide. The job of every team, then, is not just to build software, but to ensure that communication flows seamlessly. To build a common language, one where both sides are heard, and where misunderstandings don't become roadblocks. After all, at the heart of every great product is not just great code—but a great conversation.

The Empathy Gap – Understanding What's Really Being Said (and Unsaid)

Most gaps in software projects don't emerge from malice or incompetence. They come from misinterpretation. In the heat of deadlines and the weight of decisions, the smallest misunderstandings snowball into big problems. A developer saying, "This will take more time" rarely means "I'm just not that committed." More often, it's shorthand for something deeper, something essential: "If we rush this, we'll incur technical debt that will multiply costs later." A product owner saying, "We need this now" doesn't always mean "I don't care about quality." It often means, "There's a customer, a contract, or a public commitment riding on this." In both cases, the words are compressed, truncated versions of complex realities. Without empathy, those words can feel like accusations, like demands, when in reality, they are just context in need of understanding.

The problem is that, for all the technical expertise and tactical decision-making developers put into their work, they often underestimate how opaque their technical concerns sound to outsiders. A developer explaining latency budgets, build pipeline failures, or memory leaks might as well be speaking a foreign language to someone worried about customer churn or revenue losses. These are real problems, but they're invisible to those who don't live in the code. On the flip side, business leaders often underestimate how arbitrary their demands sound to developers. The urgency of "We need this by the end of the quarter" feels capricious when the underlying reason—a looming investor call, a renewal deadline, or a competitive launch—is kept silent. It's like speaking two different languages and assuming the other side will automatically understand the subtext. What's worse, neither side thinks to ask for clarification. Instead, frustration fills the gaps.

This is where empathy becomes not just a buzzword or a soft skill, but a necessary tool for survival in the complex ecosystem of software development. Empathy in software development isn't about being nice or pleasing everyone—it's about stepping outside your perspective and trying to understand the motivations behind what is being said and what is left unsaid. It's about recognizing that developers aren't the only ones under pressure, and business leaders aren't the only ones dealing with complexity.

When a developer hears urgency, the natural response should be to ask, "What's at stake if we miss this date?" Instead of assuming that "we need it now" translates to "drop everything," they should seek to understand the larger picture. When an executive hears caution or hesitation from a developer, the response should be, "What will break if we cut this corner?" The truth is, there is always a price to pay when cutting corners. Software is never just "built" and then forgotten; it's a living, breathing organism, always in a state of evolution. A small decision can create ripples that may not be visible today but will absolutely be felt tomorrow.

The real work of understanding comes from surfacing the unsaid. Developers need to understand why deadlines exist and what they mean to the business. It's not about micromanaging or asking for permission; it's about understanding the consequences of the decisions that are being made and the weight they carry. On the other hand, business leaders need to grasp that speed is not the same as quality, and that every shortcut taken is another potential defect waiting to happen. When both sides take a moment to consider the broader implications of their statements, they shift from posturing to true negotiation. The language changes from "We can't do this" and "You're stalling" to something far more productive—"How can we make this work, while minimizing risk?" The true power of empathy is that it makes room for that conversation.

In the absence of empathy, what follows is a dangerous dynamic. Developers dig in, feeling unheard, and double down on technical purity. "No, we can't do that, it will ruin everything," they say, even when a compromise might be possible. Meanwhile, managers push harder, feeling stonewalled, and double down on deadlines. "We don't have time for this," they insist, unaware of the inevitable consequences of that decision.

Neither side is lying. Both are protecting what they value, but without understanding the other side's value, it looks like defiance. With empathy, though, it becomes collaboration.

The teams that truly thrive don't eliminate tension. They channel it. They transform pressure into a shared conversation rather than a battle for dominance. Empathy doesn't erase deadlines or technical risks, but it helps them take form within a shared vocabulary, allowing for honest trade-offs. "We can ship by June, but it means skipping testing and raising the chance of outages by 40%." The facts are on the table now. "We can take three more weeks, but it means we'll miss the customer demo and risk losing the contract." Again, honesty. It's not about making everything work perfectly; it's about seeing and understanding the cost of each decision. With empathy, teams can make the uncomfortable call: which option, while imperfect, will cause the least harm? Which trade-offs are worth the cost, and which ones are too high?

Honesty, when grounded in empathy, becomes the guiding principle. It's a powerful tool, but it only works when both sides are willing to embrace it. Without it, teams are left to operate in the dark, making decisions based on incomplete or distorted information. The act of surfacing what's unsaid—not the blame, the assumptions, the fears, or the ambitions—is what allows for a decision to be made that everyone can live with. It's this ability to navigate the mess of reality, to find a shared path between competing needs, that makes for the best software teams.

In the end, the real problem with software projects isn't the code. It's the conversation around the code. It's the misinterpretation, the assumptions, the silences. The best teams aren't the ones that avoid conflict—they're the ones who can talk through it with understanding and purpose. They don't let dogma or pride block the way; they use empathy to clear the path and turn tension into meaningful action. Because the reality is, software is never just about code. It's about the people, the conversations, and the shared commitment to a common goal. When that connection happens, it's no longer just about fixing a bug or hitting a deadline—it's about creating something greater than the sum of its parts.

Documentation as a Love Language – How Clarity Fuels Collaboration

Earlier, I admitted a hard truth: Documentation rarely saves the day. In most organizations, it's often treated as an afterthought—rushed, outdated, written in a tribal dialect, or, worst of all, ignored entirely. A requirements document gets buried in Confluence, slipping to the bottom of the backlog where it fades into oblivion. API documentation rots in forgotten wikis, waiting for the next person brave enough to decipher its mysteries. Even the README that was meant to welcome new contributors turns into a time capsule—preserved but irrelevant, showing how the system looked three versions ago, before the last major refactor or update. And when documentation fails like this, it only reinforces the worst stereotypes: developers saying, "We don't have time to write things down," and the business side thinking, "Developers don't care if anyone else understands what they built."

But here's the thing: documentation doesn't fail because it's useless; it fails because it's treated as busywork, something to be done when everything else is finished—never as a true tool for communication. When written well, documentation isn't just paperwork. It's a feature. It's a contract for work completed in durable form, something that lasts beyond the project at hand. It's the bridge that carries intent and context from one team to another, from one iteration to the next, and even across future versions of the software.

Good documentation works only when it's written for someone specific—when it speaks their language and addresses their needs. It's easy to forget, especially when we're deep in the weeds of code, but the people who will use our documentation aren't us. They're product managers, designers, business leaders, and even the developers coming on board six months from now. A well-crafted document can do more than explain a decision; it can shape the trajectory of a project, creating alignment and reducing friction before it becomes a bottleneck.

For developers, documentation means code-level clarity. It's API references that explain why one method behaves the way it does, or why a particular design pattern was chosen over another. It's architecture decision records (ADRs) that document why the team chose a monolithic approach today, even though microservices may be the trendy alternative tomorrow. Developers don't need flowery prose. They need details, a map to navigate the complexities of a system that they didn't build. Without this clarity, they're left guessing, navigating by feel, with no real way to understand the decisions made before their time.

For product and design teams, documentation means context. It's not just a list of features and requirements. It's a living document that explains why trade-offs were made, why certain edge cases were ruled out, or why a particular design pattern was chosen. It's the story behind the wireframes, the journey from initial concept to final product. It's the subtle distinctions between what "done" really means and what was abandoned along the way. Without this context, even the best-designed features may miss the mark on user experience or market fit.

For business stakeholders, documentation means outcomes. It's a clear, understandable explanation of what the system does, what it doesn't do, and how it connects to customer needs or revenue goals. Too often, business stakeholders are left in the dark, staring at incomprehensible code and jargon. Documentation that translates technical detail into tangible value helps bridge that gap, allowing them to make informed decisions about the product's future.

But to make documentation work for everyone, it's essential to remember three key practices—three principles that transform documentation from a necessary evil into a genuine asset:

1. **Make it part of the workflow, not a side project.** Documentation can't be an afterthought. It must be woven into the daily process. Docs should be reviewed alongside code; decisions should be logged as ADRs when they're made—not reconstructed after the fact, long after the context

has faded. If documentation is treated as a backlog item, something to be done when everything else is finished, it rots like anything left neglected. A living document isn't a static file on Confluence. It's a dynamic record that evolves alongside the system it describes.

2. **Write for clarity, not completeness.**
   We've all been guilty of creating bloated documents—lengthy specs that aim to cover every possible edge case and scenario. The problem is, no one reads them. Nobody has the time or patience to wade through 50 pages of minutiae. A well-written two-page document that explains why a decision was made and what risks were considered is infinitely more valuable than an exhaustive encyclopedia of what could have been. Focus on reducing ambiguity, not covering every "what if" under the sun. The goal isn't completeness; it's precision. Provide just enough detail to empower the reader to make informed decisions, but not so much that it overwhelms them.

3. **Keep it discoverable.**
   There's nothing worse than well-written documentation that no one can find. If it's buried in a wiki or hidden in the depths of a repository, it might as well not exist. Link decisions to Jira tickets, embed README files at the repo root, and create a single, easy-to-access "front door" to your knowledge base. When documentation is easily searchable, properly indexed, and always up-to-date, it becomes a powerful tool—an asset that accelerates onboarding, minimizes miscommunication, and reduces the distance between teams. If documentation is neglected or hidden, it's the same as not having it at all.

But it's not just about the practical benefits; documentation is cultural. Teams that treat it as "someone else's job" end up with graveyards of half-written, outdated pages that no one looks at. Teams that embrace it, recognizing clarity as part of the craft, create rich libraries of context that can be drawn from at any time.

Documentation becomes an integral part of the development process, not an afterthought, but an essential, living piece of the workflow.

It's also about respect. Good documentation shows respect for the people who will come after you—whether they're your teammates, the stakeholders who rely on your decisions, or even your future self, who will have to remember why you made that choice when you're deep into a different problem six months from now. It's easy to forget that we write for others, not just for ourselves. And when we forget that, the documentation becomes a shield—a crutch for when things go wrong, a way to avoid responsibility. But in its best form, documentation isn't about creating a fortress around our choices; it's about making the decisions we've made accessible, transparent, and easy to understand.

Documentation, when treated correctly, isn't sacred text to be hoarded and protected like some religious manuscript. It's knowledge, and knowledge only has value if it can be shared. The irony is, if the knowledge is too precious to share, it's not documentation—it's job security theater. Documentation is about creating clarity for others. When it's done well, it opens doors instead of closing them. It becomes the scaffolding that helps teams build, improve, and adapt over time. It's not overhead. It's a deliverable. It's a sign of respect for the people who will work with your code, whether it's a teammate onboarding tomorrow, an executive making trade-offs today, or your future self revisiting this code when the world has changed around you.

If "communication is the missing API," then documentation is the part that scales. One-on-one conversations may resolve today's conflicts, but clear documentation prevents tomorrow's. When a system goes down at midday, the difference between fumbling through Slack history and following a crisp, well-documented runbook is the difference between an incident and a disaster. When a new hire joins, the difference between guessing at tribal knowledge and reading a living guide is the difference between months of floundering and a few weeks of meaningful contribution. Documentation, when treated as a first-class citizen of the development process, becomes an asset that shapes the future of the project, not just a byproduct of it.

In the end, documentation isn't a luxury; it's a responsibility. It's the love language of software development. It shows that you care enough about the work you've done to ensure that others can understand it. To help them build on it. To make sure the project doesn't stop when you walk away. When done right, documentation is the bridge between today's work and tomorrow's progress.

Chapter 7 – Culture: The Invisible Framework

Culture is not just a perk or a poster hanging in the break room; it's the default operating system of a team. It's the unseen hand that guides how people handle deadlines, reviews, failures, and success. It's there, quietly, in the choices made every day. And while no one may explicitly talk about it, culture is present in every exchange, every sprint, and every pull request. The truth is, strong culture doesn't eliminate problems; it makes them manageable. It transforms challenges into opportunities for collaboration rather than division. Weak culture, on the other hand, turns every setback into a crisis. It makes the smallest roadblock seem insurmountable.

Trust as the Primary Architecture – How Healthy Teams Outperform Brilliant Loners

You can't buy culture, you can't outsource it, and you definitely can't bolt it on after the fact. Culture isn't a feature or a set of ideals written on a whiteboard for everyone to forget. It's something that's built day by day in the choices teams make, and it's often this quiet construction that decides whether the software—and the people building it—will scale or stall. It's in the little things. How a leader responds to failure, how feedback is given or withheld, how conflicts are addressed, and most importantly, how trust is nurtured.

The strongest architecture in a software system isn't in the code—it's in the culture. The cleanest designs, the most elegant abstractions, and the best technical decisions are meaningless if the team doesn't trust each other. Without trust, the system becomes brittle. The smallest change triggers unnecessary friction, every code review turns into a turf war, and deadlines become an opportunity for everyone to bluff their way through the process. On the flip side, with trust, those same rituals transform. They become opportunities for collaboration, not combat.

Trust is the foundation for everything that follows. It's what makes feedback safe to give and to receive. It's the bedrock on which teams stand when admitting they don't know something, when acknowledging that a decision didn't work out as expected, and when pushing through problems together. Trust is also what makes it possible to ship faster—because people aren't second-guessing each other's motives. They know that everyone is working toward the same goal. The team that trusts each other escalates issues earlier, shares knowledge more freely, and carries the on-call burden without resentment.

Think about it: it's not just the code that benefits from trust—it's the entire process. With trust, developers are willing to share code. Not just in the literal sense of pushing commits, but in how they document, explain, and invite others into their corner of the system. Code is more than just lines on a screen; it's a shared responsibility. If you're the only one who understands a module, you don't just own the glory of writing it. You also own the failures that come with it when it breaks. When code is written with clarity, when it's explained well, and when the documentation is easy to follow, the burden is distributed. On-call rotations become survivable, vacations become possible, and the system gains resilience. It doesn't matter who wrote it—the entire team can own it.

But sharing code is only one part of it. The emotional side of sharing is just as important. It takes courage to hand off something you built and humility to let someone critique it. Developers often equate ownership with identity. So when a peer questions a decision, it feels personal. It feels like a judgment of their worth. But in teams built on trust, the narrative changes. The act of handing over your code is no longer an act of surrender; it's an investment in the system's reliability. It's a display of confidence that someone else can improve it, or at the very least carry it forward if something happens to you. That transfer of ownership doesn't just make the system better; it makes the team stronger. The culture is larger than any individual's ego.

Leaders have a unique role in setting this tone. Their actions speak louder than their words. When managers admit they don't have all the answers, when they own their mistakes publicly, or when they ask for feedback on their own decisions, they model the humility and courage they expect from the team. Vulnerability from a leader signals that it's safe for everyone else to be honest too—that saying "I need help" or "I was wrong" won't be punished but respected. This kind of example doesn't just stop with the leader; it cascades downward. When leaders show that they are human, teams stop pretending to be infallible. They stop acting like lone wolves and start acting like collaborators, where the focus is on finding the best solution, not saving face.

Contrast this with the corrosive effects of distrust. When developers don't trust management, they inflate their estimates, hide bad news, and morale plummets. Management's own distrust leads to more micromanagement, more processes, and more layers of approval. When there's no trust between peers, inefficiency starts to seep into every process. Duplication, defensive abstractions, and "my code vs. your code" silos replace collaboration. It's not incompetence. It's fear, plain and simple. And when fear governs the codebase, inefficiency takes root.

The mechanics of trust aren't glamorous. They come from small, repeatable actions. Leaders who own mistakes instead of spinning them. Teammates who document instead of gatekeeping. Reviewers who critique code without attacking the person behind it. These aren't grand gestures. They're habits. And like unit tests in a codebase, their value compounds over time. When a team has trust as its foundation, it knows that challenges will come. It knows that there will be moments of misalignment, of mistakes, of misunderstandings. But with trust, those challenges don't break the system. They don't unravel the team. Instead, they become an opportunity to grow and adapt.

In the end, trust is the invisible framework that holds everything together. It's not in the code diagrams, but you'll feel it in the velocity, the fluidity, and the spirit of the team. Trust makes the difference between a team that collapses under pressure and one that flexes and adapts. Good architecture in code makes systems resilient. Good architecture in culture makes teams resilient. And without both, nothing scales.

Burnout Detection and Prevention – Recognizing the Slow Fade Before It's Too Late

Trust is what allows teams to absorb stress without breaking. Without trust, when the pressure builds, it doesn't just hit the system—it hits the people. The software starts to crack, but so do the relationships. A brittle culture doesn't always falter in a spectacular crash. Often, it falters in small, invisible ways, eroding slowly from the inside out. The failure mode isn't a catastrophic outage; it's burnout. What looks like a dedicated team can sometimes be an exhausted one, slowly retreating under the weight of expectations, their energy draining until there's nothing left to give.

Burnout in software is rarely dramatic. It doesn't announce itself with grand collapses or breakdowns. It sneaks in quietly, disguised as dedication. It shows up in subtle, almost imperceptible ways: the code reviews done with a sigh instead of curiosity, the deadlines met with indifference instead of pride, once-engaged developers retreating into silence. These are the small signs—the moments where passion starts to fade. By the time someone admits they're burned out, it's often too late to undo the damage. Not just to the individual, but to the team and the product as well. Burnout is a slow fade, camouflaged as "being a team player."

The software industry doesn't help the situation. It has normalized exhaustion, framed it as proof of commitment, as if sleepless nights and overextended workweeks are the markers of dedication. Sixty-plus-hour weeks, late-night deployments, and constant "firefighting" become worn like badges of honor. But these badges aren't symbols of success—they're signs of systemic failure. Sustained overwork doesn't produce heroes; it produces attrition. Developers may still show up, still write code, but their edge dulls with every passing day. Fewer risks are taken. Fewer improvements are suggested. The code isn't being built—it's being coped with.

Detecting burnout requires a shift in perspective. Metrics like commits and tickets are helpful, but they won't tell you the full story. They won't tell you that a developer hasn't taken a vacation in over a year or that the same three people are absorbing every critical incident. The early warning signs aren't in the numbers—they're human. They're in the small changes: the rising irritability during reviews, the reluctance to volunteer for tasks, the cynicism about product decisions. These aren't personality flaws. These are symptoms of a system consuming its people faster than it can replenish them.

For developers, the hardest part of burnout isn't even acknowledging it; it's admitting it. No one wants to be the one who taps out. They're afraid of looking weak, of appearing less committed. The culture demands you push through. But the reality is, speaking up doesn't have to be a dramatic confession. It can be something as simple as flagging when the workload is no longer sustainable. It might be saying, "If we push to hit this deadline, testing will slip, and our error rate will climb." Framing the conversation this way doesn't make burnout a personal failure—it makes it an organizational liability. Burnout is a failure of the system, not the individual.

One powerful way developers can surface burnout is by making the invisible visible. It's about capturing those small shifts in behavior and calling attention to them before they snowball into bigger issues. It might mean logging incident hours, noting when "crunch mode" becomes the new default, or raising concerns during retrospectives instead of letting them fester. It's easy to dismiss a single developer saying, "I need a break" as a personal preference, but when a pattern emerges—when multiple developers bring up the same fatigue—it becomes clear that the system needs correction. The act of speaking up, especially when it's done collectively, shifts the narrative. It reframes burnout from being an individual failing into a signal that leadership needs to act on.

Preventing burnout isn't a complex task, but it's an inconvenient one. It demands honesty and courage from leadership. It requires managers to set limits rather than quietly celebrate overwork. Leaders must spread on-call rotations and ensure that no one person is carrying the burden alone until they burn out. Deadlines need to reflect real capacity, not wishful thinking. And perhaps most importantly, the culture must foster an environment where asking for a break is seen as responsible behavior—not weakness.

Burnout thrives in cultures that don't trust their people enough to believe them. When someone says they are at their limit, the response should be to adjust the load, not question their commitment. It's about creating an atmosphere of transparency, where people feel comfortable saying, "I'm at capacity," and it's understood as a sign of responsibility, not a lack of dedication. Preventing burnout isn't about wellness perks or free snacks in the breakroom—it's about structural honesty. Clear priorities, a sustainable pace, and work that has real meaning. Teams that get this right don't just avoid losing people; they gain a reputation as places where developers can do their best work without sacrificing themselves in the process.

And, perhaps, the hardest part of this all is that burnout isn't something that just shows up at work. It leaks into personal lives, too. It comes home with you. And that's when the toll becomes the heaviest. It doesn't just impact the person working the late hours—it impacts their family, their friends, their ability to disconnect. The worst part is when the developer no longer has the ability to care enough to even realize they've been walking this edge for months, or years. They may be too far in to see it.

But when it's caught early, it's a different story. By allowing space for the conversation, for the empathy, for the vulnerability, burnout can be avoided or at least mitigated. The act of listening, of seeing a fellow developer as a person first and a resource second, is what separates the companies that thrive from those that barely survive.

Burnout, in the end, isn't inevitable. It's a consequence of a system that demands too much, too quickly, without ever asking for too little in return. The teams that listen—and understand—are the ones that will build software that lasts, and people who remain healthy and engaged.

Leadership's Role in Cultural Code – Modeling Transparency and Collaboration

If trust is the framework of a team, then leadership is the operating system that determines how that framework functions. A team doesn't magically generate honesty, humility, and collaboration; these qualities are not born overnight. They are cultivated, modeled, and reinforced—or, if neglected, undermined—by the daily actions of those in charge. Culture doesn't emerge from mission statements or posters on the wall; it is built in the trenches, in every decision a leader makes, especially when things go wrong. The choices that leaders make, their ability to model vulnerability, and the way they interact with their teams in moments of failure are what ultimately shape the culture.

When leadership is solid, when trust flows freely from the top, it creates a ripple effect throughout the team. When trust is broken, when leaders act with detachment or self-importance, it doesn't just hurt the system—it slowly suffocates the people. Culture isn't something that's bolted on later; it's the air a team breathes, and it either lifts them or drags them down. When trust is cultivated, setbacks are treated as bumps in the road rather than existential crises. When trust is absent, every minor problem becomes a mountain.

Leaders who act like they have all the answers—who never admit to uncertainty—create silence, not innovation. Those who never own up to their mistakes breed fear in their teams, an environment where no one dares to speak up because they fear repercussions. And the leaders who demand transparency, yet never practice it themselves, create an atmosphere of quiet resentment, where cynicism seeps into every conversation. It's a toxic pattern, a feedback loop where truth and trust remain hidden under layers of defensiveness.

But when a leader admits failure, shows their thought process when making decisions, and invites critique, the entire team begins to understand that transparency is not a weakness—it's a strength. When leadership practices transparency, it becomes a practice the whole team adopts. Being open about what decisions were made, why certain trade-offs were necessary, and what risks were involved, only strengthens the leader's position. It doesn't diminish their authority; it solidifies it. Leaders who can show their reasoning, who can expose their vulnerabilities, and who can acknowledge when they don't have all the answers set the stage for others to follow their example.

True collaboration is something leaders must model—not just demand. Leadership is not about micromanagement. It's not about overseeing every step of the process and controlling every decision. Instead, it's about rolling up your sleeves to understand the constraints your team faces, asking questions before issuing directives, and being present in the process without suffocating it. The most effective leaders are those who create room for their team to breathe, for their team to contribute, and for their team to grow. They understand that collaboration isn't a box to check—it's a fundamental part of how work gets done.

This is where humility becomes non-negotiable. It isn't just about technical leadership or business acumen; it's about having the courage to admit when you're out of your depth. Leaders need the humility to say, "I don't know," and the wisdom to let someone else—someone smarter, someone more specialized—take the lead when the situation calls for it. That isn't weakness; it's strength. True leaders understand that their role is not to be the smartest person in the room, but to surround themselves with the best talent and give them the resources to thrive. As Antos Parrish wisely put it: "The best leaders are those most interested in surrounding themselves with assistants and associates smarter than they are. They are frank in admitting this and are willing to pay for such talent."

A leader who clings to their own importance hoards not just knowledge but credit as well. They stifle the potential of their team. But a leader who practices humility multiplies both knowledge and credit across the entire team. They build a culture of collaboration, where success is shared, where mistakes are learning opportunities, and where the team, as a whole, rises together.

The impact of leadership on culture is recursive: Leaders set the tone with their actions, and those actions become norms within the team. Those norms then become part of the invisible framework that determines how the team responds to stress, conflict, and failure. A culture rooted in transparency and collaboration doesn't guarantee that a team will avoid failure—it doesn't mean bugs won't get shipped or deadlines won't be missed. But in a healthy culture, those failures become steppingstones to improvement, not reasons for blame. The team is better equipped to handle the inevitable bumps in the road because they've built resilience through trust.

Leadership doesn't just set the direction; it sets the tone. And the tone—the way leadership communicates, reacts, and sets examples—is what determines whether a team builds resilience or quietly burns itself out.

Culture is what defines how a team handles stress, conflict, and failure. But even the healthiest culture needs the right scaffolding—the right processes and tools—to keep things moving smoothly. The danger comes when we mistake tools and processes for culture itself. Project management tools alone don't make a team collaborative. Stand-ups don't inherently make a team aligned. Continuous integration and deployment (CI/CD) pipelines don't guarantee discipline. At best, tools reflect the culture that wields them; at worst, they become a form of theater that hides dysfunction.

Leadership sets the tone, and processes set the tempo. If the leadership is tuned to collaboration, transparency, and humility, the tempo will match. Processes and tools will serve the team, reflecting its values and reinforcing its resilience. If leadership fosters distrust, micromanagement, and inflexibility, the tools and processes will reflect that too, becoming a burden rather than a benefit.

Ultimately, it's the relationship between leadership and culture that determines a team's success. A team that trusts its leaders and each other is far more likely to succeed—not because they're perfect, but because they can adapt, learn from mistakes, and come together when challenges arise. The right leadership is the foundation that allows this dynamic to thrive, and from there, the team can build something that scales—not just in the work they produce but in how they collaborate and grow together.

Chapter 8 – Processes and Tools Without the Buzzword Fatigue

Every tool in the modern developer's kit holds the dual nature of both essential ally and inevitable frustration. They are supposed to make things easier, to streamline processes and increase productivity. They are supposed to provide reliability and allow us to move at scale. But in practice, they often come with their own set of obstacles, bringing more pain than promise. It isn't that these tools are inherently bad—although some definitely are—it's that they slip too easily from being powerful leverage to becoming an overbearing liability. They are like scaffolding; necessary, yes, but the moment you start serving the scaffolding instead of letting it serve the building, you're no longer constructing software. You're simply maintaining ceremony.

The Tools We Love (and Love to Hate) – Version Control, Testing, and CI/CD Realities

Modern software development, for better or worse, is constructed on a foundation of borrowed code. This borrowed code comes from countless third-party libraries, frameworks, and open-source tools. These frameworks save months—if not years—of development time. A few lines of code, something that a team of developers spent weeks perfecting, can suddenly be replaced by a one-liner imported from an open-source library. The initial promise is efficiency, and in many ways, it delivers. But the unspoken cost is something that lingers, hidden beneath the polished interface. Every borrowed piece of code comes with its own baggage: hidden bugs, security vulnerabilities, dependencies you can't control, and upgrade paths that are out of your hands. It's a precarious dance, relying on code written by strangers who are often well-meaning but may not even be aware of the impact their work has on the ecosystem.

Consider the Heartbleed [3] vulnerability in OpenSSL, a vulnerability that demonstrated to the entire world just how dangerous this dependence can be. An unnoticed flaw in a widely used library compromised security across the internet for years. Despite that, we continue to rely on open-source projects because the alternative—building everything ourselves—is a cost too great to bear. We trust in the generosity of other developers, even as we know that the next open-source library might carry its own unseen risk.

Package managers, like npm, Maven, PyPI, and NuGet, were introduced to help manage the vast dependencies that came with this new world of open-source code. These tools made it possible to scale our systems quickly, to draw from a vast well of ready-to-run code and reuse it as if it were our own without having to rewrite vast amounts of functionality. But this convenience also comes with its own set of frustrations. Managing these dependencies, keeping them up to date, and ensuring their stability becomes a full-time job in itself. A simple application might now rely on hundreds, even thousands, of packages. The trade-off is clear: we've exchanged the time it would take to write bespoke code for the fragility of an interconnected web of dependencies.

The open-source movement, as well, has deepened this paradox. Open-source code is supposed to be a victory for freedom and collaboration. But it's also become a battleground for developers who debate not just the features of a tool but its ideological underpinnings: the license, the governance model, and even the politics of "free" versus "open." Choosing a library isn't just about its technical merits anymore; it's about whether it aligns with your team's philosophy, whether you want to support its community, or whether you want to make a political statement about the dangers of commercial software. We've allowed tool selection to turn into an ideological choice, and in doing so, we've traded objectivity for idealism.

This ideological commitment to open-source solutions has led many teams to reject commercial options outright, even when those paid options might be better suited to their needs. There's a kind of pride in rejecting commercial solutions, as if making a purchase order for a paid tool somehow signals weakness or compromise. But what was once a practical decision—using open source when it's mature and well-supported—has transformed into an identity statement. And that identity is costing us the freedom to make rational, business-driven decisions. The result? Tools are judged by their alignment with our ideology, not by how well they serve our business needs.

This bias shows up in postmortems all the time: "We chose the open-source version because it was free," followed by, "We now spend two full-time developers maintaining and patching it." The cost of ownership doesn't vanish just because a tool is free; it simply shifts from a budget line in procurement to hidden payroll within the development cycle. Those unpaid hours, the time spent troubleshooting obscure bugs, the slow, grinding process of maintaining something that was never meant to be a full-fledged solution—these are costs we don't see until they're buried in the backlog. "Free" isn't free when it carries with it additional staff time, incident responses, and opportunity cost.

Despite all these challenges, we continue to adopt tools that promise much but deliver inconsistently. Why? Because the alternative—the act of reinventing everything ourselves—is far more unappealing. Developers will tolerate flaky libraries, poorly documented frameworks, and the endless string of minor issues with tools that solve 80% of the problem. Why? Because the cost of building those last 20% of the solution from scratch would be far greater. So we accept the mess. We put up with the brokenness because the benefits—however imperfect—are still far better than starting from zero.

This is the eternal trade-off we face: leverage versus liability. Every tool, every framework, every library offers a degree of leverage—an ability to move faster, to do more with less. But that leverage always comes with a hidden liability—the bugs, the security holes, the dependency hell, the abandonment. As developers, we are in a constant balancing act, weighing the value of what a tool offers against the cost of what it brings with it. In the end, we are all just trying to make the best of a complex, interconnected system that's never perfect but always necessary.

The tools may frustrate us, but they are the scaffolding that holds our systems together. We rely on them, even when they frustrate us. We embrace them, despite their flaws, because they allow us to scale. Yet, the true challenge lies in how we select and use these tools. It's not enough to simply adopt the latest shiny framework or the most popular library. We must remember the trade-offs involved, recognize when our reliance on tools is growing into a problem, and take active steps to minimize the liabilities while maximizing the leverage. Only then can we truly build something that lasts, that scales—and that doesn't collapse under its own weight.

The Human Side of Tooling - Ownership, Burnout, and Bureaucracy in Your Processes

Tools aren't just technical; they shape how teams collaborate, how they struggle, and, ultimately, how they succeed—or fail. The right tool can make teamwork feel almost effortless, creating a seamless flow of work. But the wrong tool? It can wedge people apart, putting up barriers between teams, departments, and even the developers themselves. Project management tools, for example, are the most obvious offenders. Loved by managers for the visibility they provide and hated by developers for the bureaucracy they impose, these tools are not inherently evil. The problem lies in the disconnect between measuring progress and actually making it.

A tool that promises to enhance productivity can quickly become a burden if it adds unnecessary layers of complexity or forces teams into an unwieldy workflow. It's not the tool itself that creates friction, but how it's integrated into the team's daily routine. For instance, a slick tool that's supposed to streamline project management might end up consuming more time with its rigid workflows and mandatory updates than it actually saves. The moment a tool becomes more of a ritual than a resource, it stops driving success. Instead of the team using the tool to achieve their goals, the team starts serving the tool, trying to meet its demands rather than their own.

At the heart of the matter lies developer experience. The technical power of a tool doesn't matter if it's painful to use. Developers are quick to abandon clunky, frustrating pipelines in favor of simpler, less feature-rich solutions if it means less mental overhead. Even if a tool can do everything right, if it's difficult to use or doesn't feel reliable, it won't stick. Developers are pragmatic, and they will naturally avoid friction where they can. A tool that is easy to adopt, intuitive to use, and, most importantly, reliable, becomes part of the team's muscle memory. It becomes ingrained into their workflow and their daily routine. It's not just another piece of tech; it's something that enables the team to do their best work.

The friction that stems from bad tooling can erode morale. When the tools are difficult to use or don't mesh with the way the team works, it doesn't just waste time—it also breeds frustration. And frustration is a quiet killer of productivity and enthusiasm. Developers are forced into workarounds, trying to find shortcuts and solutions that get the job done but avoid the pain that comes with the tool itself. The result? A system of hacks and temporary fixes that patch over the tool's shortcomings instead of solving the underlying problem. This not only adds more work in the long run but also undermines the system's integrity. Over time, this stress can wear a team down and lead to burnout.

The culture of a team can be heavily impacted by the tools they use. Tools can centralize power, as we see with systems that are overly complex and opaque. A brittle pipeline or an outdated tool, for instance, can concentrate knowledge in the hands of a few specialists. In this setup, the people who know how to fix things become invaluable but also overloaded. The team relies too heavily on a few key individuals, and if they're unavailable or leave, the system can collapse. That's a form of reverse hostage situation. On the flip side, well-documented, accessible tools empower the entire team. They create a sense of shared ownership and reduce burnout because the responsibility is no longer resting solely on the shoulders of a few.

Transparent tools allow for greater collaboration and help distribute the load. They make systems more resilient because no single failure point is locked away in the mind of one person. When knowledge is shared, the team feels more united, and the pressure on individuals becomes more manageable. Conversely, when teams aren't able to understand the tools they're using, burnout becomes more prevalent. It's harder to maintain energy and enthusiasm when every task requires relying on someone else to fix a critical component of the system. Over time, this lack of autonomy can build frustration and fatigue, leading to a silent attrition as developers disengage and stop caring.

Keeping tools up to date is yet another treadmill that teams can't seem to escape. It's easy to fall behind, even slightly, and suddenly your "stable" toolchain becomes a ticking time bomb. Security patches get delayed, APIs deprecate, and suddenly something that seemed reliable is now a liability. But staying on the bleeding edge isn't the answer either—constant churn introduces its own headaches. Developers have to spend valuable time adjusting to updates, integrating new features, or replacing deprecated components. It's a balancing act: Staying on top of updates without falling into the trap of constantly fighting fires. The sweet spot is elusive, where teams stay boring where they can, innovate only where it truly matters, and accept the reality that "hot-swappable" workflows are more of a fantasy than a reality—yet another contradiction in the domain of software development.

Customization versus standardization is yet another balancing act. Customization allows a tool to fit perfectly within the team's existing workflow, adapting it to their exact needs. But this comes at a cost. Custom setups create unique workflows that no one else understands, locking the team into a fragile, bespoke environment. Standardization, on the other hand, promotes consistency and interchangeability, but it forces the team to adapt to tools that might not perfectly align with their needs. Customization gives flexibility but locks you in, while standardization offers stability but takes away adaptability. Every team eventually learns this lesson: the more you customize, the more you own forever.

The tools we use are a reflection of our processes, our culture, and ultimately, our team's success. When we use the right tools, in the right way, they amplify our efforts, driving us to do better work and collaborate more effectively. When we use the wrong tools, or use them poorly, they not only waste time but also create friction that damages the very culture we're trying to build. Tools are not neutral. They either enable collaboration or they make it harder. They either distribute responsibility or concentrate it. And, as with everything in software development, they are only as good as the people who use them. If we want tools to truly serve us, we need to be mindful of how we choose them and how we integrate them into the systems we build. Because at the end of the day, the tools should be helping us build better software—not just getting in the way.

Beyond the Present - Tools in an AI-Driven World

The next wave of tooling is already here, and it's transforming the way we work: AI copilots, code generators, and automated reviewers that promise to turn developers into "force multipliers." These tools, powered by artificial intelligence, offer promises of speed and efficiency—autocomplete for boilerplate code, suggestions for fixes, and even the ability to refactor entire classes in a fraction of the time it once took. For some, this feels like liberation. The mundane tasks are handled by machines, leaving them free to focus on the creative and complex work that requires human thought. It's a tantalizing future where software development is streamlined, automated, and exponentially more productive. But for others, the rise of AI in development is a creeping threat, a signal that the work they've spent their careers honing might soon be reduced to something obsolete, something that can be done by a machine. In their minds, AI is the first step toward de-skilling, towards disposability.

The real question isn't whether AI will write code—because it already does. The real question is how teams will balance the automation offered by AI with the oversight and creativity that human developers provide. Blindly trusting an AI to stitch together complex dependencies might speed up the process, but it also creates a faster path to shipping vulnerabilities. And on the flip side, rejecting AI outright is equally shortsighted. It's already embedded in our workflows, and its capabilities are expanding rapidly. We can no longer afford to ignore it, nor should we blindly embrace it. The most productive middle ground is to see AI as scaffolding—a tool to accelerate routine work, not a replacement for the thoughtful, human-driven process that ensures the integrity of the system.

As we move further into the AI-driven future of development, the tools we use won't be a choice between humans and machines. Instead, the most successful teams will design workflows where humans and machines complement each other, working together in harmony to amplify the strengths of both. This vision requires new thinking: tools that remain interchangeable, observable, and reversible. Teams will need to design systems where any component—AI assistants, build pipelines, test harnesses—can be swapped out and replaced without unraveling the entire operation. It's a future where flexibility and adaptability are paramount, and where technology serves to enhance human ingenuity rather than replace it.

The challenge ahead isn't just about inventing new tools or embracing new technologies. The hardest challenge for the industry will be keeping those tools boring enough to be dependable, flexible enough to evolve, and humane enough to support the people who rely on them. In this new world, software isn't just built by tools. It's built by teams of people, and the best tools are the ones that stay out of the way, letting the humans do what they do best. This doesn't mean that tools shouldn't evolve or that innovation should be stifled. Rather, it means that we must embrace a balanced approach—one that allows for innovation without overwhelming the foundation of trust, collaboration, and integrity that every good software system requires.

At the end of the day, the best AI-driven tools will not replace developers; they will make developers better. They will eliminate the mundane and repetitive tasks, giving developers more time and cognitive bandwidth to focus on the problems that truly require human creativity and judgment. The tools will evolve, but the core of what makes good software will remain unchanged: a deep understanding of the needs of the business, an intimate knowledge of the system's architecture, and a commitment to maintaining the integrity of the code. AI will not write all the code. But it will help developers write the better parts of it faster, and with fewer errors.

Tools, at their best, are like the hidden scaffolding that makes a tall building possible. You don't see them once the structure is complete, but without them, the structure would never have stood. This is the future of tooling in an AI-driven world: not tools that replace the developers, but tools that elevate the developers, allowing them to build software faster, more reliably, and with more room for the kind of creativity that machines cannot replicate.

But even as we lean into AI and embrace the evolution of our tools, it's crucial to remember that we are the ones designing these systems. And like any tool, AI will only be as effective as the hands that wield it. It will never replace the need for human insight, empathy, and understanding. So while AI may change the landscape of software development, the human element will always be at the core of it. After all, no machine can replace the ingenuity of a team working together towards a common goal.

And so, as we look ahead, it's not the AI that should worry us. It's whether we'll be able to maintain the balance: to ensure the tools remain helpful scaffolding, rather than becoming a cage of convenience that stifles creativity and forces the human element to step aside. The future will demand adaptability, but also a firm commitment to what makes us human. Our tools may evolve, but our need for meaningful collaboration, innovation, and the deep satisfaction of solving problems together remains unchanged. It's not about making tools that can do everything for us. It's about making tools that help us do what we do best.

How to Choose the Right Tools - Good Tools Disappear into the Background

If there's one lesson from the endless parade of dependencies, package managers, CI/CD struggles, and ideological tool wars, it's this: The right tool is rarely the "perfect" one. Perfection is an elusive myth in the world of tooling. The truth is, the perfect tool doesn't exist—not in the way we'd like it to. What you're really choosing when you pick a tool is a set of trade-offs. Speed versus stability, flexibility versus consistency, free versus supported, automation versus oversight. And pretending that one tool will solve every problem is a trap. It's easy to get caught in the cycle of searching for the ideal solution, only to realize that the real question is how to balance these competing priorities.

Choosing the right tool requires stripping away the noise and returning to first principles. The key question is simple but powerful: does it solve the problem we actually have?

Too many bad tool choices begin with teams solving the wrong problem. It's a well-known pitfall—teams grab a shiny new framework, hoping that it will magically solve their scaling issues, when the real bottleneck is something much simpler like the lack of a reliable caching mechanism. Or they adopt a trendy testing suite to look disciplined, when the real problem is poor communication between teams. It's easy to get swept up in the buzz of the latest tool or technique, but the first step is always brutally pragmatic: Does this tool actually improve our delivery, stability, or security today? Anything beyond that is just noise, a distraction from what needs to be done now.

The next filter for tool selection is perhaps the most underrated: Is it mature enough to be boring?

Cutting-edge tech is seductive, no doubt. It's exciting, and it promises the kind of innovation that can change everything. But the reality is that bleeding-edge tools are often fun to demo and painful in production. They look great in a presentation, but they quickly unravel when they're subjected to the stresses of real-world use. Open-source CVEs—critical vulnerabilities exposed in widely used libraries—are a perfect reminder of why boring matters. Even something seemingly mundane can harbor catastrophic flaws. But there's also a reason why the "boring" tools tend to endure: They're stable, they've been tested in the wild, and they have strong community support. They may not be the most glamorous or the most innovative, but that's the point. They work, and they work well. When your team doesn't have the time or expertise to carry the pager for a bleeding-edge tool, it's better to opt for something dull and reliable. Glamor fades fast when it's 2 a.m., and your site goes down, and there are only two maintainers on GitHub who know exactly why but can't fix it fast enough.

Next comes the crucial question: can it be swapped out later?

No tool should be a one-way door. Lock-in isn't just about licensing; it's about entanglement. Tools are the scaffolding of development, but they shouldn't be the foundation. If you're writing code directly against a vendor's API with no abstraction layer, you're setting yourself up for future pain. You might get the initial integration done quickly, but you've now tied yourself into a solution that's difficult to change later. Are you creating custom scripts that only one person understands? Are you baking pipeline steps into a convoluted setup that no one can easily modify or replicate? The smartest tool choices leave room for flexibility. Even if you never need to switch, knowing that you could—without unraveling everything—is a form of insurance. The best tools are the ones that allow you to evolve, not the ones that force you to be stuck in place.

Now, here's the more human side of tool selection: does it make the team faster, clearer, or more aligned?

A tool is only as good as the effect it has on the people using it. This is where the rubber meets the road. You can have the most powerful tool in the world, but if it creates more confusion than clarity, it's useless. Jira is a prime example: For executives, it's a way to track progress and visibility. For developers, it's often a ticket-churning nightmare. It's not the tool itself that's the problem—it's the way it's used. CI/CD, too, can feel like a dream until it becomes a black box, with only one person knowing how to tweak it when something breaks. A good tool increases clarity. Everyone on the team can see the same truth, whether it's in the code or the build pipeline. It increases speed, helping teams ship safely and faster. It fosters collaboration, spreading ownership instead of bottlenecking it with a few individuals who hold the keys. If the main beneficiary of the tool is a slide deck, rather than the people doing the work, you've chosen the wrong tool.

These aren't purely technical questions. They're deeply cultural. Tools shape the work, but they also shape how people interact. A brittle toolchain creates bottlenecks, individual heroes, and burnout. A smooth toolchain spreads knowledge, makes collaboration effortless, and builds developer confidence. At their best, tools disappear into the background, allowing the people to do their work. At their worst, they become the work. When tools become a crutch, they impose an extra layer of process on top of the team, making it harder to get things done. It's not about the tool itself; it's about how it fits into the workflow and how it affects the team's ability to execute efficiently and collaboratively.

That's the real test: does it help people do the work, or just add layers of process around it?

Because, in the end, tools don't build software—developers do. It's important to remember that every tool, no matter how sophisticated, is still just a means to an end. The true craft lies in the hands of the developers, the people who take the tools and make them work together to create something meaningful. The best tools are the ones that disappear into the background, allowing developers to focus on the problem at hand, not on wrestling with the tool itself. This is the essence of choosing the right tool: it should empower the developer, not get in their way. Let the tool do its job—so the developers can do theirs.

And so, as we look beyond the present, beyond the hype, it becomes clear: The most effective tools are those that support the team's mission, make their lives easier, and fit naturally into the rhythms of work. Tools that make teams work faster, smarter, and more cohesively will always be the most valuable. It's not about the newest technology or the most advanced automation. It's about finding tools that just work—and allowing the human ingenuity of the team to shine through.

Chapter 9 – The Developer's Skill Stack

At the core of every software developer's journey lies a hard truth: it's not just about the code. Strip away the tools, the titles, and the theater, and what you're left with is the developer's skill stack. Not the buzzwords, not the résumé keywords, but the actual capabilities that determine whether a project succeeds or fails. These skills aren't just technical—they're human. They live in the space between knowing how the code works and knowing how to make it work in the messy reality of teams, deadlines, and shifting goals.

Technical Mastery vs. Soft Skills – the Dual Competencies That Define Success

Developers often love to pretend their value resides in the technical. The languages, the frameworks, the performance tricks—these are the things that feel tangible, the concrete evidence of a developer's prowess. They shine in interviews, on GitHub, and in technical forums. But when you look closely at the projects that fail, most didn't collapse because the team couldn't reverse a linked list or fix a bug in their SQL queries. No, they failed because people couldn't align. They couldn't communicate. They couldn't set aside their egos long enough to make the necessary trade-offs together.

The term "soft skills" is misleading, even insulting. They're not soft, and they're definitely not optional. The ability to communicate, negotiate, and show empathy isn't just a nice-to-have. It's what turns a developer from someone who delivers code into someone who delivers outcomes. Communication, collaboration, conflict management, and empathy these aren't HR buzzwords or vague ideals. In the trenches of a project, they are survival tools.

Take communication, for example. A developer's ability to explain technical risks to non-technical people without condescension or jargon is essential. It's about knowing how to say, "This deadline isn't realistic" in a way that invites conversation instead of defensiveness. It's the skill to translate system constraints into business impact, making the technical world accessible and understandable for others. Bad communication, on the other hand, is mumbling about latency, technical debt, and obscure frameworks until the executive team tunes out. A developer who can translate technical concerns into language the business can understand is an invaluable asset. It's not just about sounding intelligent, but about ensuring everyone is on the same page, moving toward the same goals.

Collaboration is another key competency that defines success. In an ideal world, everyone on the team would be self-sufficient. But in the real world, the lone-wolf archetype rarely works. The reality is that "your code" is never just "your code." It's part of a larger system, and that system is the shared responsibility of everyone on the team. At scale, silos create fragility. The more isolated each piece of code is, the more it becomes a point of failure. Successful collaboration is about shared ownership, knowledge transfer, and honest code reviews. It's about building trust, not just dependencies. A culture of collaboration doesn't just improve the product; it strengthens the team. When developers communicate openly and share their knowledge freely, the team becomes more resilient, and the software becomes stronger.

Then there's conflict management, which is an underrated superpower. Developers disagree—about architecture, process, priorities, even naming conventions. Disagreement is inevitable, but how those disagreements are handled is what sets apart the successful teams from the failing ones. Skilled developers can argue fiercely, hashing out trade-offs and debating options, and then walk away from the table with a shared understanding. They don't let the argument fester into personal resentment or organizational politics. Poor developers let the argument spiral, and what was once a discussion about the best approach becomes a personal feud that undermines progress. Conflict, when handled correctly, can lead to deeper insights, better decisions, and a stronger team dynamic. When handled poorly, it can fracture the very foundation of the project.

But perhaps the most important skill of all is empathy. Empathy isn't about being nice or agreeable; it's about accuracy. It's the ability to understand not just the words, but the intent behind them. It's the ability to hear, "We need it by Friday," and instead of dismissing it as arbitrary, ask, "Why is this deadline critical? What's at risk if we don't meet it?" Empathy allows developers to probe the reasons behind decisions, to question the assumptions behind every demand, and to understand the stakes. It transforms every interaction into a negotiation instead of a confrontation. When empathy is lacking, every request feels like an imposition, every deadline like an arbitrary constraint. With it, trade-offs become visible, and solutions become negotiable. Developers and managers alike can better align, and together, they can navigate the complexities of a project with a shared understanding.

Another vital skill is teaching and mentoring. There's an old saying: "Knowledge is power," but in the world of software development, the real power lies in sharing that knowledge. A developer who hoards knowledge is a bottleneck. A developer who shares their knowledge creates resilience. The long-term health of a system depends less on who wrote the cleverest abstraction and more on whether the next person can understand it. Teaching and mentoring aren't just for the "senior" developers. They're an essential part of every developer's job. Every developer, no matter how experienced, should pass down their knowledge, whether it's in a code review, a pair-programming session, or even in casual conversations. It's this sharing that builds a culture of trust, knowledge, and continuous improvement.

None of this is meant to diminish the importance of technical mastery. You can be the world's best debugger, the fastest coder, or the most skilled at navigating complex algorithms. But if you can't explain your fix, document your process, or ensure the team doesn't repeat the same mistakes, you've only solved half of the problem. Technical mastery without soft skills produces brittle systems and a toxic work environment. The industry is full of brilliant jerks and charming incompetents, both of whom are detrimental to the team and the project.

The real professionals—the ones everyone quietly wants on their team—are the ones who can straddle the divide. They understand the intricacies of architecture, and they can explain it to the CFO without triggering an aneurysm. They can mentor juniors without turning it into a hazing ritual. They can argue fiercely about trade-offs, lose, and still commit to the decision. Technical skills will get you through the interview; soft skills will keep you on the team.

In the end, it's the balance of both that makes a developer effective. It's the technical mastery that drives solutions, but it's the soft skills that ensure those solutions are meaningful and sustainable. It's the ability to code, but it's equally the ability to collaborate, to communicate, and to grow together. The best teams understand this balance and live it every day. They know that software isn't built in isolation—it's built in community. And it's the humans behind the code, the ones who understand the technical and the personal, who make it all work.

Problem Solving as a Core Currency – Beyond Syntax to Systems Thinking

"There is nothing so useless as doing efficiently that which should not be done at all." – Peter Drucker

At the heart of software development lies an often-overlooked truth: Code is not the job. Solving problems is. Code is just the artifact—the evidence that some piece of logic was made explicit, that a solution was crafted, and that a problem was addressed. That's why syntax is often overrated, and problem-solving is frequently undervalued. Syntax can be memorized, borrowed, or auto-completed. But problem-solving? Problem-solving requires judgment. It requires the ability to interrogate vague requirements, spot hidden constraints, and navigate trade-offs without drowning in endless options. Problem-solving is the *art* of making choices when clarity is absent.

Most failed projects don't fail because the code was bad. They fail because the team solved the wrong problem with great efficiency. Think about the CRM system that was built to capture a thousand data points, only to find that salespeople refused to enter any of them. Or the "scalable" platform that was designed to handle millions of users—when the product was struggling to manage a thousand. The developers in both cases wrote solid, even elegant code; they just optimized for irrelevance.

Strong problem-solvers ask the questions others skip:

- What is the actual outcome we're chasing?
- What evidence do we have that this feature even matters?
- Are we fixing a symptom (slow queries) or the underlying disease (bad data modeling)?
- What trade-offs will haunt us six months from now?

This discipline demands systems thinking. Most problems don't live in isolation—they're nodes in a messy web of dependencies. A performance issue might be rooted in business rules, not just queries. A scaling crisis might trace back to a sales promise made under tight pressure, not necessarily a flaw in infrastructure. Real problem solvers see these connections. They know that a bug fix isn't always just about the code; it can be a reflection of a product decision gone awry. And sometimes, a product decision is just a manifestation of a deeper strategic flaw.

But here's the irony: The best problem solvers often look "slow." They resist the urge to code their way forward. Instead, they pause, they breathe, they reflect. In organizations where velocity is worshipped, this looks like foot-dragging. It feels like hesitation. But that pause? That's where the real value lies. It's in that space where clarity is achieved, where the right question is asked, and where the problem is reframed. A day spent reframing the problem can save a year of building the wrong solution, of chasing the wrong goal, of wasting resources on irrelevance.

Problem-solving is a kind of organizational arbitrage—a dance between the business world and the technical world. It's about translating messy, undefined business goals into tractable technical designs. And then, just as importantly, translating those technical constraints back into business impact. It's the art of navigating complexity and aligning divergent priorities. Anyone can learn the syntax of a language. Far fewer can walk into a meeting where requirements are contradictory, politics are thick, and deadlines are absurd, and walk out with a solution that's not just technically sound, but one that everyone can agree on, align behind, and rally around.

That's why problem-solving is the core currency of software development. It compounds. Good solutions make the next problem easier to solve. But bad ones? They metastasize into technical debt, brittle systems, and sleepless nights. They build up until they become the structural weakness that everyone has to work around. In the end, it's not the number of lines committed that matters—it's whether the problems that mattered were actually solved. Whether the team avoided making small mistakes that grew into big ones, whether they found the right path instead of wandering aimlessly down dead ends.

This ability to solve problems with insight, to think beyond just the code, to constantly ask the right questions, is what separates good developers from great ones. It's not just about knowing how to write clean, concise code. It's about understanding the system within which the code exists, and how it interacts with everything else. Good developers know the syntax, the tools, the abstractions—but the best developers know how to ask, *"Is this what we really need?"*

And it's the teams that solve the right problems, at the right time, that build the software that stands the test of time. Those teams understand that technical mastery alone doesn't solve the problem. The solution isn't just in the code. It's in the thinking that goes into the design. And that thinking, that judgment, is the most valuable thing a developer brings to the table.

The real job of a developer isn't just to write code—it's to figure out how to make the right decisions, understand the complexities around those decisions, and translate them into something actionable, scalable, and meaningful. That's why problem-solving is the core currency. It's the skill that compounds. It's the one that makes a difference.

Impostor Syndrome and Adaptability – Thriving in Constant Change

"It is not the strongest of the species that survives, nor the most intelligent, but the one most adaptable to change." – Charles Darwin

There's a paradox woven deeply into the fabric of software development: The more you learn, the more you realize that mastery is an ongoing journey. Every new framework, language, or architectural pattern feels like an invitation to greatness, yet it quickly becomes a reminder that your knowledge has an expiration date. Once, you might have thought you had a grasp on the state of the art, but as quickly as you master one thing, something else changes—another language pops up, another tool gets popularized, another paradigm is discovered. In this ecosystem, proficiency doesn't last forever, and the reality is that it's often measured in months.

The result? Impostor syndrome. This quiet undercurrent that flows through the veins of almost every developer. It strikes when you look around, see your colleagues seeming to understand it all, and feel, with sudden dread, like an outsider in a room full of experts. The familiar feeling creeps in: "I'm going to be exposed any minute now. I don't belong here." And yet, if we were honest with ourselves, we'd realize that *everyone* feels this way at some point. The people we think have it all figured out? They don't. They're just as insecure as we are, navigating the same sea of shifting technology, unsure whether they're swimming or sinking.

The thing about impostor syndrome is that it isn't the flaw we often think it is. It's not something to erase or overcome entirely. In fact, it's a signal. It's a sign that you're still learning, still stretching, still growing. The more you doubt, the more you leave space for growth. Self-doubt isn't a weakness; it's a necessary part of the process—and, when managed properly, it acts as a check on overconfidence. The real risk isn't acknowledging what you don't know. The real danger lies in pretending that you know everything. Developers who can acknowledge gaps in their knowledge open the door to faster learning, better collaboration, and, crucially, fewer costly mistakes.

It's hard to admit we don't have the answers, especially in an industry where success seems to demand that we have all the answers, at all times. But the most valuable teams aren't the ones with the most "expert" knowledge—they are the ones that embrace adaptability. Being adaptable, being able to pivot when necessary, and being open to learning something new is often more important than having the deepest well of knowledge.

The world of software moves quickly. Today it's microservices, tomorrow it's serverless, the next day it's AI-generated code. In a year, the whole landscape could have changed again. What doesn't change, however, is the developer's ability to adapt—to absorb new information, discard old habits, and adjust course under pressure. The best developers, the ones who thrive in this chaos, aren't the ones who cling hardest to what they know. They're the ones who can pivot without panic, who can learn without ego, and who can embrace change with the same enthusiasm as stability.

Take, for example, the Java developer who once dismissed JavaScript as a "toy," only to realize too late that the web had shifted beneath them. Or the seasoned C++ veteran who resisted Python, thinking it was a fad, until they discovered its potential in machine learning. The survival skill isn't knowing which language is most popular right now—it's about embracing what's necessary to solve the problem and being willing to pick up new skills when the need arises.

In this industry, survival isn't about what you know today; it's about how quickly you can adapt tomorrow.

But tools and skills alone aren't the full story. They exist within processes—some formal, some chaotic—whether it's the rigid structure of waterfall or the freedom of agile. Before we dive into lifecycles and delivery models, it's important to acknowledge a sobering truth: No matter how skilled you are, no matter how much you know, even the best developers can be undone by a broken process. Process doesn't just support the work; it shapes it, molds it, often in ways we don't expect. And that, perhaps more than anything, is where the real challenge lies—navigating the parade of methodologies while maintaining focus on what really matters.

This adaptability, this willingness to let go of yesterday's assumptions, is what separates developers who just survive from those who thrive in the face of constant change. It's not about memorizing every new framework or learning the latest library just to keep up—it's about knowing which tools to use, when to let go, and when to pick something up that might just change the game. And the only way to know that? You have to be willing to learn continuously, even when you're unsure.

Chapter 10 – The Lifecycle and the Circus

Project management in software has always been a bad imitation of other industries. Manufacturing counts units produced, construction pours concrete—you can literally watch progress rise from the ground. In software, progress looks like staring at a screen while nothing works until suddenly it does. Estimating timelines is closer to fortune-telling than scheduling, because debugging one "simple" issue can take five minutes or five weeks, and nobody knows which until it's over. That uncertainty breaks the illusion that traditional methods can tame the chaos, which is why we keep reinventing "flexible" approaches that promise control but usually just rebrand the same confusion.

Models That Made Us – Waterfall, Agile, RAD, and Their Hybrids

Every few years, the software industry rediscovers project management, as though it's a brand-new invention. The same trade-offs that have been part of our DNA for decades are rebranded, recast, and slapped with fresh labels. We print them on glossy slides and convince ourselves that this time—this method—will save us from missed deadlines, bloated budgets, and demoralized teams. The reality is that lifecycles have less in common with science and more with theater. Waterfall was supposed to bring order and discipline. Agile was sold as the liberator from inflexible processes. RAD promised rapid prototyping and speed, while hybrids were hailed as pragmatic solutions. Instead, they've all collapsed into a circus act: clowns juggling deadlines, ringmasters demanding ever-expanding scopes, and tightrope walkers balancing precariously on the wire of "done."

The methods themselves aren't inherently flawed. They're just frameworks, after all. The act begins when organizations mistake frameworks for guarantees—when they confuse ritual with real results. A two-week sprint won't rescue a team that struggles with poor communication. A requirements document won't magically align business stakeholders with engineers. Process doesn't eliminate the hard parts of building software; it merely reshuffles where the bodies are buried.

Waterfall, born out of the cold, calculated world of defense contracting, was meant for a different time. Predictability mattered more than adaptability. Requirements were seen as static and fixed. But when the method encountered the chaos of the real world, its fatal flaw became painfully clear: It assumed that requirements could be known upfront and remain immutable. Take the infamous example of the Denver Airport baggage system—six years late, hundreds of millions over budget, and eventually scrapped.[5] The rigidity of the process froze complexity before it was fully understood. Waterfall couldn't bend to accommodate the growing complexity of the system it tried to define, and it was overwhelmed by it.

Agile was born out of this frustration. It promised flexibility, iterative improvement, and user-centric design. At least, in theory. In practice, many companies adopted Agile like a new diet fad, keeping the sugar but calling it "low carb." Stand-ups became mind-numbing status dumps. Sprint planning turned into negotiation poker where developers felt the heat of "must deliver by Friday" rather than a shared commitment to collaboration. Retrospectives devolved into group therapy, with no real action items. When Spotify's Squad model [6] was published, companies quickly adopted it by copying the org charts but missing the culture and context that made it work in the first place. The result? "Agile" in name, bureaucracy in practice.

Then there's Rapid Application Development (RAD), which promised salvation in speed. Prototype everything, ship fast, evolve later. It sounded perfect—especially for startups eager to move quickly and gain market share. The problem? Prototypes often became production systems, and the rapid iterations that were supposed to be an asset ended up becoming their downfall. Many dot-com companies died not because they couldn't raise funding, but because they mistook duct tape for design. The code was fragile, the systems buckled under real-world pressure, and "iteration" turned into a constant firefighting mission.

So, what about the hybrids—the middle ground? SAFe [2], LeSS, Wagile—an alphabet soup of compromise. These frameworks were supposed to bring the best of both worlds, but in reality, they often delivered the worst of both: Waterfall's paperwork with Agile's ceremonies, consultants pocketing the difference. Many large enterprises now proudly proclaim to be "Agile at scale" after adopting SAFe, but developers often joke that it's really just "Waterfall with more meetings." The circus stayed; it just changed costumes.

The deeper issue, though, is that these project management systems are built on the fantasy that complexity can be tamed by process. These frameworks assume that requirements are stable, people are predictable, and communication flows cleanly from the top down. But reality is messier. Requirements shift mid-stream. Incentives misalign. Stakeholders pull in opposite directions. Frameworks collapse because they try to turn human judgment into checklists, mistaking ceremony for coordination, and documentation for alignment. What kills projects isn't using the wrong model; it's the misguided belief that the model itself can shield you from the inevitable trade-offs.

The lesson is as unglamorous as it is vital: No lifecycle model will save you. These frameworks are guidelines, not talismans. What really matters is whether leaders can resist turning frameworks into theater, and instead use them as scaffolding for real judgment, context, and genuine delivery. Even when the method fits and the team executes with discipline, the true battle rarely comes from the process itself. The real fight comes from the gravitational pull of ambition.

Take Denver's doomed baggage system or the infamous Healthcare.gov [7] debacle. Both projects may have followed their respective models to the letter, and still, they collapsed under the weight of just one more requirement. A well-followed method may look good on paper, but the real struggle is surviving scope creep—that relentless, unseen pressure pushing projects past the limits of their original design.

The spectacle continues, but the core challenge remains: mastering the art of survival in an environment where the methods may change their costumes, but the performance stays the same.

Scope Creep Survival Tactics – Managing Ambition vs. Delivery

Scope creep is often dismissed as a byproduct of poor planning or management, but in reality, it's much more insidious than that. It's a law of nature, one that seeps into every project and stretches deadlines and resources beyond recognition. It starts small, almost innocuously: a feature request here, a slight tweak there. But before long, the original vision is buried under layers of demands that weren't part of the original plan. The thing about scope creep is that it doesn't just grow; it metastasizes, often in ways that make you question if you ever really had control of the project in the first place.

Take the case of Healthcare.gov [7] in 2013. The original scope, ambitious as it was, seemed achievable. The government set out to create a platform that would serve millions of Americans—an important and necessary task. But somewhere along the way, the well-intentioned vision spiraled out of control. Politics got involved, contractors threw in their requirements, and various agencies added their own touches. What began as a complex but manageable system morphed into a bloated behemoth, and the eventual launch collapsed under its own weight. It wasn't just the scale that failed—it was the lack of authority, the inability to say no, that led to a two-billion-dollar lesson on what happens when scope creep is allowed to go unchecked.

Yet not all scope creep is malicious. Often, it's driven by shifting market realities or unforeseen needs. Sometimes compliance regulations change overnight, forcing teams to scramble for solutions they hadn't anticipated. Or maybe a competitor launches a feature that makes your product seem outdated before you even have a chance to finish your roadmap. It's easy to blame these external factors, but the real danger arises when these additions are accepted without acknowledging the cost.

The myth of "we'll add this feature and still hit the deadline" is the most common form of wishful thinking in the software industry. It's fantasy accounting that leads teams down a dangerous path of perpetual late nights and unfinished features. The clock keeps ticking, but deadlines slip further and further away.

So, how do you survive scope creep when it feels inevitable? It comes down to discipline—and the ability to say no.

Anchor scope to outcomes. Every feature, every addition, every tweak should be tied directly to a measurable outcome: revenue, user retention, or risk mitigation. Anything that doesn't fit into this framework is a distraction, a nice-to-have that doesn't justify its weight. Anything else is indulgence. The danger comes when teams start accumulating features for the sake of appearances, for the sake of looking busy. This only dilutes the product's value.

Force explicit trade-offs. This isn't about cutting corners or delivering half-baked solutions; it's about being realistic. Adding new scope should mean cutting something else or admitting that the delivery date will need to shift. Otherwise, you're simply making a promise you can't keep. Pretending otherwise only sets the project up for failure.

Budget for change. It sounds simple, but it's rarely done. A roadmap without any contingency is a roadmap that's already on the path to failure. Change is inevitable—whether it's due to market shifts, unforeseen challenges, or new opportunities. The key to managing this change is to bake flexibility into your timeline, budget, and expectations. When the inevitable happens, the team can adjust without feeling like the world is caving in.

Write everything down. Scope creep thrives in informal conversations, quick Slack threads, and hallway discussions. It thrives in ambiguity, where no one has clearly defined the trade-offs or clarified the impact of the changes. It's easy to forget what was discussed on a Friday afternoon when the pressure mounts on a Monday morning. In the heat of a project, it can feel like just another quick conversation—but paper beats memory when the blame game begins. Writing everything down is a defensive measure, one that saves time and frustration down the line. It provides clarity and helps prevent the creeping fog of misalignment from turning into a full-blown disaster.

Surviving scope creep isn't about pretending that it can be eliminated entirely. It will always be there, lurking at the edges of a project, ready to sneak in unnoticed. But it can be contained. The teams that succeed in the long term are the ones who understand that saying "no" isn't a career-killer, it's a professional skill. Every project will face scope creep at some point, but it's the teams that manage it effectively that will still deliver. Those who fail to manage it will find themselves trapped in a never-ending cycle of misaligned priorities and half-finished products.

In the end, it's not just about surviving scope creep; it's about managing the tension between ambition and delivery. The greater the ambition, the more carefully you need to tread. Without discipline, scope creep turns into a monster of your own making, one that swallows deadlines and distorts the original vision until you're left wondering how you got so far off course.

The art of survival is knowing when to say no, when to prune the excess, and when to focus solely on what matters most.

From Vision to Version – Steering Projects from Start to Ship

The grand visions are seductive. They promise the world. They show a shimmering future full of possibilities. Slide decks are crafted, filled with optimistic projections of what could be: disruption, transformation, and hockey-stick growth. Everyone in the room nods in agreement, a little buzzed from the possibilities. But the truth is, no product ships as a "vision." It ships as version numbers—incremental releases, iterations, and the messy reality of getting something out the door. The discipline isn't in dreaming big; it's in cutting scope down to something that's testable, maintainable, and, most importantly, shippable.

Take the example of Windows Vista. Microsoft's promise was nothing short of revolutionary. It was supposed to be a new era in user experience, a system that would change how we interacted with computers. The vision was lofty, ambitious even. But that vision morphed into a decade-long delay and a bloated operating system that shipped with major flaws. By the time it arrived, Vista didn't feel like an upgrade—it felt like an afterthought. The features didn't line up with the promises, and users were left disappointed. It wasn't the vision that failed—it was the mismanagement of it, the failure to reduce the scope and focus on what could actually be delivered on time and with real value.

Now contrast that with Amazon Web Services (AWS) in its early days. AWS was a revolutionary shift, no doubt, but it was minimal in its first form. The product was clunky, far from perfect, but it was real. It was out in the world, providing tangible value even if it wasn't the fully fleshed-out, polished solution it is today. The version was the bet, and it paid off because Amazon delivered something that customers could use, while continuing to improve upon it. It wasn't about creating the perfect, all-encompassing vision. It was about solving real problems with real solutions—releasing those versions and iterating.

Shipping software isn't a ceremony; it's more like steering. Every release is a bet, a calculated wager. You bet that the current feature set is valuable enough, that stability is at a sufficient level, and that the debt you've accumulated won't sink the team. But these bets don't get easier as you grow. Take Facebook's mantra of "move fast and break things [1]." That worked when the platform was simply a place for college students to share pictures. It was a clever mantra—almost rebellious—but once Facebook became a global infrastructure, it was reckless. The stakes changed, and what was once seen as an innovative philosophy quickly became a liability. So, they had to evolve, retire the old philosophy, and replace it with something that could hold up under the pressure of being a critical service used by billions.

From version 0.1 to 10.0, the pattern is largely the same. You'll ship incomplete work, miss dates, and inevitably accumulate debt. The key question isn't whether these things will happen—it's about how you handle them. The real test is whether you manage those inevitable failures openly, deliberately, and honestly. The difference between a circus and a professional craft is that in the latter, everyone knows exactly where the risks are, and they understand the costs. They don't pretend that everything will work as expected. They prepare for failure and deal with it as it comes.

The tension between process and reality will always exist in software development. You can write all the models you want—Agile, Waterfall, RAD, or whatever the latest trend is. They all promise order. But reality? That's always messy. It's unpredictable. Teams, people, clients—all of these human elements throw wrench after wrench into the works. And so, the frameworks—however shiny or well-meaning—are just scaffolding, not solutions. The *method* you choose isn't going to change the fact that people still need to communicate, still need to understand each other, and still need to make hard decisions.

The teams that succeed in the long term aren't the ones who treat frameworks as law. They're the ones who know when and how to adapt. Use methods lightly, treat them as lines in the sand, not laws. A few practical rudders can help guide the ship, but rigidity is a recipe for disaster.

Here's how to steer the chaos:

Favor clarity over ceremony. Every ritual, whether it's a stand-up or a sprint planning session, should have a purpose. It shouldn't be there for the sake of having something to do. If a stand-up adds no value, shorten it. If it's only becoming a formality, cut it out. Clarity matters more than ticking boxes.

Tie process to outcomes. Every document, every meeting, every tool used should have a direct connection to outcomes. Is it contributing to revenue? Is it reducing risk? Is it delivering more value to the customer? If the answer is no, then it's just pageantry.

Expose trade-offs openly. If you want to maintain trust, you need to be transparent about trade-offs. You can't have it all—deadlines, costs, and quality all have their limits. Make those trade-offs visible. Write them down, make them explicit, and allow everyone to understand the consequences. This is how alignment happens.

Keep processes reversible. Nothing is permanent—not the methods, not the tools. Processes should be flexible enough to scale back or swap out as conditions change. The *lock-in* mentality doesn't just apply to technologies; it applies to processes, too.

Protect human judgment. This is the most important anchor of all. Frameworks, processes, tools—none of them have the nuance, the judgment, or the context that people do. Allow space for human discretion and adaptability. Frameworks can guide, but only humans can make the decisions that matter.

Software will always exist in the tension between ambition and constraint. Between vision decks and version numbers. The healthiest organizations don't try to eliminate that tension—they learn to navigate it. They acknowledge the circus for what it is and choose to steer the chaos instead of pretending it can be eliminated.

And yet, the circus never stops. The next act is already being built: AI copilots promising acceleration, sustainability mandates reshaping priorities, and career bets shifting as hype cycles collide with long-term relevance. The question isn't whether these things will change the rules. The real question is whether we can tell the difference between spectacle and substance when the next big thing arrives.

The show will go on, but how we steer it—that's the true test.

Chapter 11 – The Future: Beyond the Code

The future of software isn't just messy diagrams and hype–it's AI-generated code, open source propping up products with volunteer labor, and "green tech" mostly confined to slide decks. Every breakthrough seems to bring as much liability as it does progress. The challenge now is whether we can avoid repeating the mistakes of the past while shaping a future that serves more than just the balance sheet.

Industry Trends with Real Impact – AI, Ethics, and Sustainable Tech

Artificial Intelligence (AI) has evolved at a breakneck pace. What was once a futuristic dream tucked into the corner of "someday" slide decks has now become an integral part of the daily workflow for developers. From autocomplete features in code editors to sophisticated systems that can draft entire applications or refactor complex codebases in seconds, AI has seeped into the core of software development. It can write boilerplate APIs, complex UIs, detect bugs, and even predict potential security flaws, often faster than a human could. For some, this feels like the liberation they've been waiting for, a break from the monotonous and tedious parts of coding. But for others, it feels more like a slow erasure of their craft—a de-skilling wrapped in the shiny veil of innovation. Both views are valid. The productivity gains are undeniable, and yet, so are the risks.

The unsettling truth isn't that AI can generate code. The real concern is that it can also generate liability, just as easily as it can draft a perfect API. Algorithmic bias, opaque decision-making processes, and code lifted from dubious or unreliable sources all end up under your company's logo. And when a model inadvertently leaks customer data, or amplifies an already-existing bias, it's not the AI that faces the consequences—it's the organization and usually not even the individual developer who accepted the pull request. Compare that to the realm of civil or mechanical engineering, where accountability is more concrete, with licenses, ethics boards, and liability frameworks designed to hold individuals responsible for their work. In the world of software, that accountability remains abstract, elusive, almost invisible. A breach that leaks millions of user records typically ends with a press release or a public apology, not with a developer facing disbarment or legal consequences.

The same selective accountability exists in the realm of sustainable tech. Every vendor with a public image has at least one slide in their presentation about carbon awareness, renewable energy, and reducing environmental impact. But real change? That's rare. In fact, thanks to the increasing demands of AI-powered data centers, we're actually consuming more energy than ever before and reversing carbon-neutral commitments in the name of progress.[8] Developers might optimize build pipelines for faster tests, improving efficiency on the surface, but optimizing for lower energy usage rarely makes it to the backlog. Green computing—a noble concept—is often reduced to little more than a marketing veneer. It's not yet the engineering discipline it needs to be. The only real motivator for change comes when data center bills rise, or when regulators step in to impose stricter mandates.

And yet, the uncomfortable truth remains: Developers are still accountable. Whether they admit it or not, if you paste AI-generated code into your production pipeline and ship it, you are the one who owns it. Courts won't care that GitHub Copilot wrote that function. They won't care that ChatGPT suggested the regex pattern. Bugs, vulnerabilities, and biased algorithms don't come with disclaimers or get swept under the rug. They will still fall under your company's name, and you will be held responsible. When something goes wrong—whether it's a bug that causes a critical failure, an algorithm that discriminates, or an entire system that collapses under load—the consequences come down on the people who shipped it. AI may be in the driver's seat, but you are the one holding the steering wheel. The autopilot won't get blamed when the plane crashes.

The future of software development isn't going to be defined by the next trendy framework or the hottest coding language of the moment. The real question, as we look ahead, is how we're going to build the equivalent of professional guardrails around the tools we now wield so eagerly. Ethical constraints, sustainability mandates, and accountability structures need to become integral to our processes. These are the frameworks that need to evolve alongside the technology, because if we're not careful, AI-generated nonsense will become the focus of tomorrow's outages, bugs, and lawsuits. The stakes are too high for us to pretend that the systems we build don't have consequences, especially when they are intertwined with our lives, our data, and our infrastructure.

But the discomfort doesn't end with AI alone. The same accountability gaps appear when we lean too heavily on open-source software. Open-source is the backbone of so much of what we build today—an incredible, collective effort from countless developers around the world. While most OSS projects have yet to outlive their authors, it's a system propped up by unpaid maintainers, fractured communities, and fragile dependencies. These are the unsung heroes, the invisible scaffolding of modern software. The problem is, when those libraries and tools break, when they go unmaintained or become unreliable, we don't always know who to turn to for accountability. Critical systems that companies rely on could crumble, leaving entire industries vulnerable to failure.

This dependency on open-source software often feels like a silent risk that most organizations don't want to confront. The reality is that it's too easy for companies to outsource their infrastructure needs to these communities without fully grasping the long-term implications. What happens when that widely used library becomes abandoned? When the maintainers can't keep up, or worse, they're forced to stop working on it altogether? Who is accountable when something breaks? Most companies continue to run with these tools because they're convenient, they're cost-effective, and they offer incredible flexibility. But it's only a matter of time before the cracks show.

The time to think about the long-term impact of these decisions is now. We have a responsibility to nurture the systems we depend on, whether they're AI models, open-source frameworks, or entire networks of software. And we need to start asking the difficult questions about the risks we're taking. Who will bear the burden of these decisions when they fail? Who will take responsibility?

As the software industry barrels into the future, the tools and technologies that fuel our work will continue to evolve, and so will the complexity of the decisions we make. The question isn't whether AI, ethics, or sustainability will shape the future—it's whether we, as developers and stewards of this technology, can navigate these new realities with the accountability and foresight they demand.

The rules are changing, and we have to be ready to meet them head-on. It's not just about coding smarter; it's about developing with ethics, accountability, and sustainability as foundational principles. The tools we use may continue to advance, but the responsibility we carry will only grow. The real question remains: can we distinguish between spectacle and substance in this ever-evolving world of software? And when we can't—who will step in to hold us accountable?

Open Source: Gift or Gamble? – The Promise and Perils of Collaboration at Scale

In the world of software, open source stands as both the backbone and the Achilles' heel. It's the lifeblood of modern technology, fueling everything from the simplest web apps to the most complex AI-driven platforms. Yet, it's also the very thing that makes the industry so vulnerable. For every revolutionary leap, like Linux or TensorFlow, there's a disaster waiting in the wings—vulnerabilities like Heartbleed [3] or Log4j [9] that catch us off guard, exposing not just the software but the systems built around it. These open-source tools, born of collective effort, sometimes crack under the pressure of that very scale. We're building the infrastructure of tomorrow on volunteer labor and amateur maintenance, and yet we act shocked when it creaks under the weight.

The mythology around open-source software is one of freedom. It's an idea that we're all part of something bigger, that anyone can contribute, improve, and build without the constraints of corporate red tape. But the reality is far messier. With freedom comes obligation—someone has to patch the bugs, write the docs, and maintain backward compatibility. Too often, the community treats backward compatibility as optional and documentation as a luxury. Libraries break APIs like a competitive sport, leaving downstream teams scrambling to fix problems they never saw coming. We praise the freedom to fork and customize but ignore the fragmentation that results. Standards? Rare. Governance? Inconsistent. And sustainability? Well, the usual model is "hope that a Fortune 500 company steps in to write a check."

The problem extends far beyond isolated libraries or rogue projects. Modern software doesn't just depend on open-source—it depends on dependency trees so vast and intertwined that no team truly understands them. A single npm package can bring in hundreds of indirect dependencies, many of which are maintained by unpaid volunteers or hobbyists, each one a potential time bomb waiting to explode. The left-pad incident was the first real wake-up call—an innocuous little package, just a few lines of code, that brought down thousands of projects when it was deleted. A small mistake led to big consequences. And as we continue to build on this ever-expanding network, supply chain attacks now target the very tools we rely on, finding new ways to exploit a system that was supposed to be secure. The risk isn't hypothetical; it's systemic. What used to be the scaffolding we trusted for speed and flexibility has slowly become one of the biggest threats to our stability and security.

Meanwhile, companies gorge themselves on open source like it's an all-you-can-eat buffet. They take what they need, implement it wherever they can, and only throw a bone to the maintainers when PR optics demand it. The cost doesn't disappear by avoiding licensing fees—it shows up as hidden labor, often unpaid, as developers scramble to maintain what's been borrowed, never truly contributing back to the very projects that keep them running. The responsibility still rests on the shoulders of those using open-source tools, but more often than not, it's out of sight and out of mind.

Looking forward, the future of open source isn't about more projects, it's about fewer, healthier ones. Sustainability in this space means companies need to pay for what they depend on—either through direct sponsorships, support contracts, or funding foundations that ensure the long-term viability of the software. Communities must embrace governance models that treat backward compatibility as discipline, not a courtesy. And developers—those who are truly the stewards of these projects—need to start viewing their open-source dependencies not as "free" but as financial instruments. Every package is a bet: a bet on the maintainers, a bet on the ecosystem, and a bet on survival. And like any good portfolio, it needs to be diversified, monitored, and pruned. If you're not managing your open-source portfolio, it can drag your entire project down without warning.

This kind of stewardship won't come easily, but it's necessary for the longevity of the systems we're building. As we continue to rely on these tools, we must ask: Are we taking responsibility for what we depend on, or are we simply hoping the system holds up on its own? The future of open source demands more than simply consuming it. It calls for contributing back, for maintaining, for improving, and for acknowledging the consequences when it fails. Because when those dependencies break, they won't be the only thing that cracks.

Building a Career that Outlasts the Hype – Strategies for Relevance and Resilience

For developers, the future is not defined by which tool to master next, but by how they survive the churn. In an industry where every cycle introduces a new "essential" skill, the real challenge isn't about staying on top of every trend—it's about surviving the constant shift, about remaining relevant when the landscape keeps tilting under your feet. Today's buzzword is tomorrow's obsolescence and résumé gold can quickly become just another line of forgotten history. Every few months, the next tool is crowned king—anointed by blogs, conferences, and overenthusiastic marketing—only for it to be dethroned once the hype cycle shifts again.

The true key to survival in the tech world isn't in the race to master the latest thing. It's about resilience. It's about cultivating habits that last longer than any trend—practices of continuous learning, critical thinking, and adaptability that don't expire with each passing season. Careers based on chasing the newest shiny object always feel unstable. But those built on habits—those are the ones that endure.

This anxiety, this fear of being left behind, is often framed as the "AI apocalypse." People fear that the rise of code-generating systems will make developers obsolete. But the answer to this threat isn't in outcoding a machine; it's in doing the things that a machine can't. Sure, AI can do 80% of your coding. But it doesn't yet negotiate trade-offs, explain risks in complex systems, or align features with business goals. The developers who thrive in this environment will be the ones who turn AI into leverage, using it to handle the mundane, to accelerate the trivial, while reserving judgment, creativity, and accountability for the tasks that really matter—the ones that ultimately determine whether a system succeeds or fails.

Adaptability remains the most durable skill a developer can possess. This means having enough technical breadth to pivot as trends evolve, while also possessing deep enough technical depth to continue offering value. But adaptability isn't just about technical skills—it's about the softer, yet equally vital skills: communication, problem framing, and collaboration. These are the skills that won't depreciate with the next JavaScript fad. These are the skills that keep you relevant, no matter what version of the framework du jour is being touted.

If you want to survive, you need a plan. The practical strategies for navigating this shifting landscape are far less glamorous than slick portfolio pages. They are grounded, sustainable, and, most importantly, real.

1. **Build a balanced portfolio of skills**. Develop deep expertise in one stack but maintain a working knowledge of others. Stay curious and be proactive about learning what's next.

2. **Invest in soft skills**. Technical prowess will always matter, but the ability to explain trade-offs to a CFO, or to collaborate across teams, will outlast every new framework that comes along. Learning to communicate complex technical issues in a way that everyone can understand is a career-long asset.

3. **Contribute visibly**. Whether it's through open-source work, internal mentorship, or even writing—actively demonstrating your judgment and decision-making process makes your competence visible. It's about establishing a reputation that's built on how you solve problems, not just the lines of code you've written.

4. **Plan for obsolescence**. Assume that your current toolkit will be outdated in five years. Build habits that make learning part of your everyday work, not something you struggle to fit in between projects or in the wee hours of the night.

5. **Stay connected**. Communities, meetups, and networks matter just as much as certifications. Building relationships in the industry means having people who can vouch for your work and help you stay ahead of the curve.

In the end, the best career insurance isn't in the tools you use today—it's in the people who remember you for your competence, not just your commits. A career based on resilience rather than chasing every fad will withstand whatever the future throws at you.

But adaptability alone will not be enough to address the growing demand for accountability in the software industry. As more critical infrastructure becomes software-powered—airlines, hospitals, banks, governments—there's a rising demand for a standard of care that goes beyond moving fast and breaking things. As code becomes a backbone of daily life, society is beginning to ask: why aren't the people writing this code held to the same standards as the engineers who design bridges or the doctors who prescribe medicine?

Imagine a world where developers were licensed like doctors or lawyers. Not with a weekend boot camp certificate, but a legitimate professional credential. Annual ethics training. Periodic re-certifications. Continuing education—just like lawyers earn Continuing Legal Education (CLE) credits. A governing body with authority to suspend or revoke licenses when negligence leads to failure. On the surface, this idea might sound absurd. But consider the reality: Software is already at the helm of systems that manage flight schedules, control pacemakers, and clear financial trades. At that point, the absence of a license doesn't look like freedom—it looks like negligence disguised as innovation.

Creating a credible framework for developer licensing wouldn't be difficult. Start with baseline education: not just algorithms and language understanding, but system safety, ethics, and risk assessment. Implement apprenticeships that pair developers with licensed professionals—just like civil engineers or medical residents train under supervision. Mandate continuing education that keeps pace with emerging threats, such as AI, security, and privacy, not just the latest framework fad. Create an ethics board with the authority to investigate failures that put lives or critical infrastructure at risk. Tie liability to individuals as well as corporations so that "the system failed" isn't an acceptable excuse anymore.

This system would be scalable across levels. A general practice license might allow developers to work on consumer-facing applications with minimal public risk. For more critical systems—such as aviation, healthcare, or government infrastructure—higher certifications, such as "critical systems licenses," would be required. Oversight wouldn't guarantee perfection, but it would ensure a baseline of competence and accountability, ensuring that the developers who build systems like these are held to the same standards as the professionals who build bridges or planes.

This framework already has the faintest outlines in place. The IEEE offers software engineering certifications, and organizations like ACM publish codes of ethics. These efforts are just starting to evolve into something more formal. They're voluntary now—ignored by most and carrying little weight outside of résumés—but they provide evidence that it's possible. However, without teeth, without real consequences for negligence or incentives for compliance, they remain symbolic. They offer a glimmer of what might come: standards, continuing education, and accountability that could one day be elevated from "nice to have" to "mandatory."

And all of this circles back to where we started in Chapter 1. We laughed at the title inflation that turned coders into "engineers" overnight, borrowing prestige from civil and mechanical engineering without importing the discipline that comes with it. We wanted the gravitas but not the guardrails. But if we're serious about being "engineers," we can't keep playing dress-up. The accountability that comes with that title is the missing piece. Regulation is coming—whether we want it or not. The only real question is whether we, as an industry, build this scaffolding ourselves, or whether legislators, after the next catastrophic outage, impose it for us. It's clear which path is more painful. The industry has already shown it can't govern itself.

Chapter 12 – Conclusion: Nothing's Wrong and Everything's Wrong

Software is the only industry where billion-dollar products and billion-dollar outages can be delivered with the same straight face. We've built a profession where titles are inflated, productivity is confused with exhaustion, and architecture veers between napkin doodles and PhD dissertations. "Best practices" harden into brittle rituals, and every step of the way, the people doing the work are expected to carry both the code and the illusions stapled to it.

None of it is fatal in isolation. Not the buzzwords, not the frameworks, not even the occasional catastrophe. The real damage comes from pretending these contradictions don't exist, from glossing over the messiness with a smile and a "this is fine" approach. And yet, we all fall into it—the pressure to perform, to please, to get the job done at whatever cost.

Every chapter in this book has traced the same pattern: A concept starts as common sense, becomes distorted by incentives, and ends up weaponized against the very people it was meant to help. We've seen it in productivity metrics, which turn into performance theater, in architecture that morphs into résumé-driven design. Agile has mutated into bureaucracy with better stickers, and tools that promise leverage have metastasized into liabilities. Through it all, the people doing the work have been asked to bear the weight of not just their tasks, but of every flawed assumption layered on top of them.

What's broken isn't the people. Developers are not broken, and businesses are not uniquely malicious. What's broken is the industry's reflex to mistake ceremony for substance. We've convinced ourselves that the right methodology, the right tool, the right title, or the right AI assistant will finally eliminate the hard parts. But the hard parts aren't going anywhere. The trade-offs, the contradictions, the judgment calls—the fact that every decision is a balance between what's good enough and what's ideal—these are the work. They are the essence of what we do.

If there is a way forward, it lies not in seeking perfection, but in seeking proportion. Projects succeed when people resist the urge to overbuild or underbuild, when they measure progress in outcomes instead of outputs. When they remember that culture quietly outpaces process in shaping results. Too many teams have focused on the process and forgotten the people behind it. But it is the people—those who navigate the inevitable messiness with clarity and adaptability—who make things work, no matter how often the ground shifts beneath them.

Tools and frameworks should fade into the background, not take center stage. The best tools are the ones that disappear when they are used correctly, and the best practices are the ones that evolve naturally to meet the unique challenges of the team. But in the frenzy to streamline and standardize, we forget that real work happens in the tension between vision and reality. It happens when people admit the contradictions, recognize the trade-offs, and work together to make progress anyway.

The truth is, software will not get easier. The contradictions won't disappear. But the work becomes less absurd when we stop pretending they can. When we acknowledge that the noise and the hype will always be a part of the landscape, we choose to work with what really matters, with purpose and intention. Code will rot, tools will age, and buzzwords will fade away. But what endures is the choice to build in a way that matters, to create something useful, reliable, and resilient enough to survive long after the slides and slogans have been forgotten.

That, in the end, is what's "wrong" with developers—and what's also right. We are bound by the very contradictions that make our work challenging, yet those same contradictions give us a reason to care, a reason to keep improving, and a reason to believe that our best work is still ahead of us. And that's the only thing that makes the work worth doing. The ability to rise above the noise, to hold steady when the rest of the industry is spinning itself in circles, and to create something that outlasts the hype, the trends, and the noise.

References

[1] Move fast and break things - background and evolution: https://en.wikipedia.org/wiki/Move_fast_and_break_things_(motto)

[2] SAFe is Not Agile: https://jeffgothelf.com/blog/safe-is-not-agile/

[3] Heartbleed (CVE-2014-0160) - NVD entry: https://nvd.nist.gov/vuln/detail/CVE-2014-0160 and overview: https://heartbleed.com/

[4] Forsgren, Humble, Kim - Accelerate (IT Revolution): https://itrevolution.com/product/accelerate/ and DORA research: https://dora.dev

[5] Denver International Airport automated baggage system - overview and sources: https://en.wikipedia.org/wiki/Denver_International_Airport#History

[6] Henrik Kniberg - Spotify Engineering Culture (caution on copy-paste adoption): https://www.youtube.com/watch?v=4GK1NDTWbkY

[7] HealthCare.gov rollout analysis - Wikipedia overview with sources: https://en.wikipedia.org/wiki/HealthCare.gov

[8] IEA - Data centres and data transmission networks: https://www.iea.org/energy-system/buildings/data-centres-and-data-transmission-networks

[9] Log4Shell (CVE-2021-44228) - NVD entry: https://nvd.nist.gov/vuln/detail/CVE-2021-44228